M000096811

SECTS,

LOVE, AND

ROCK & ROLL

EXPERIENCES *in* EVANGELICALISM

edited by CHRISTOPHER J. KELLER *and* ANDREW DAVID

The Experiences in Evangelicalism series offers forays into the evangelical experience, rethinking and reimagining key questions, practices, and tenets of faith, as they have been framed in the evangelical tradition. Through theological reflection, critical analysis, and personal narrative, the series seeks to craft a more authentic and engaging evangelical spirituality. This series is a working partnership between *The Other Journal* at Mars Hill Graduate School and Cascade Books.

Sects, Love, and Rock & Roll

My Life on Record

JOEL HENG HARTSE

CASCADE *Books* · Eugene, Oregon

SECTS, LOVE, AND ROCK & ROLL
My Life on Record

Experiences in Evangelicalism 2

Copyright © 2010 Joel Heng Hartse. All rights reserved. Except for brief quotations in critical publications or reviews, no part of this book may be reproduced in any manner without prior written permission from the publisher. Write: Permissions, Wipf and Stock Publishers, 199 W. 8th Ave., Suite 3, Eugene, OR 97401.

Cascade Books
An Imprint of Wipf and Stock Publishers
199 W. 8th Ave., Suite 3
Eugene, OR 97401

www.wipfandstock.com

ISBN 13: 978-1-60899-327-7

Published in partnership with *The Other Journal*, Seattle, Washington.
www.theotherjournal.com

Cataloguing-in-Publication data:

Heng Hartse, Joel.

   Sects, love, and rock & roll : my life on record. Joel Heng Hartse.

   Experiences in Evangelicalism 2

   x + 188 p. ; 23 cm.

   ISBN 13: 978-1-60899-327-7

   1. Rock music—United States—Religious aspects—Christianity. 2. Popular music—United States—Religious aspects—Christianity. I. Title. II. Series.

ML3921.8.R63 H25 2011

Manufactured in the U.S.A.

To my parents

with thanks for their gifts of music and faith
and apologies for the swear words

Contents

RIYL (recommended if you like): creative nonfiction, scenes and un-scenes, "Hell" by the Squirrel Nut Zippers, boozy Canadian indie rock bands and the gospel, resisting grand histories, patriotism, the conflation of music and religion, microphone checks

RIYL: records, great moments in gospel music, Michael W. Smith, small-town Montana, Jesus Freaks, attempts at U2-like bombast, the golden age of Christian rock, *CCM Magazine* and CCM heretics, Larry Norman, Frank Black, horse tranquilizers, the Electric Prunes

RIYL: Christian radio, being eleven years old, *Blood Sugar Sex Magik* by the Red Hot Chili Peppers, Top Forty radio, the Manhattan Transfer, being punched in the throat, Altered Beast, Genesis, the Great Christian Ska Wars

RIYL: the worst band name ever, Jesus T-shirts, Catholic rock, hanging out with the wrong crowd, Billy Corgan's salvation, unforeseen erections, not having sex, regrets, speaking in tongues, evil desserts, demonic music

RIYL: fundamentalism, Audio Adrenaline, fake bootlegs, betrayal, *CMJ*, forbidden ecumenical teenage romance, Elliott Smith, *Good Will Hunting*, death wishes, breakups, love

RIYL: online pregnancy tests, Dungeon of Doom, *The Net*, libraries, Johnny Q. Public, lying on the Internet, aspiring to work in the Christian music industry, Napster, songs on computers, losing your record collection

Acknowledgments

I extend my sincere gratitude to the editors and writers who have published, praised, or otherwise encouraged me—in small ways they may
be unaware of—and helped me to believe that I could do something
like this. Thank you Ryan Pangilinan, Kate Wiley, Jonathan Kiefer,
Becca Costello, Luke Baumgarten, John Jeremiah Sullivan, Patton
Dodd, Ted Olsen, Mark Moring, Greg Wolfe, Mary Kenagy Mitchell,
Laurel Snyder, Peter Manseau, Christopher Frizzelle, Adam Gnade,
Jeffrey Overstreet, and Michaelangelo Matos. Many thanks, also, to
my friends with whom I have played and loved music: Kevin, Matt,
Andrew, Nathan, Gwen, Jon, Johnny, Kevin, Vin, and Daniel. Thanks
also to all Hengs, Hartses, Thurlows, and Soos for hospitality, love,
and support. Huge thanks of course to my parents, and to Kendal,
for being such a supportive sibling even though you barely made
it into the book. I owe a huge debt of gratitude to Andrew David
for being such a tireless and caring editor, and to Chris Keller for
encouragement and exhortation, and to everyone at *The Other Journal*
and Cascade Books for their help putting this book together. And of
course, I would not be able to do anything without the love and support of Sarah, who I love and totally want to have babies with.

The following material is used by permission:

Portions of chapter 6 are adapted from "God and Guitars," *Killing
the Buddha*, August 21, 2006. Online: http://www.killingthebuddha
.com/mag/confession/god-and-guitars/. Used by permission under
the Creative Commons Attributions License.

Portions of chapter 7 are adapted from "That Our Unity Will One Day Be Restored," Good Letters: The *Image* Blog, July 29, 2009. Online: http://imagejournal.org/page/blog/that-our-unity-will-one-day-be-restored. All rights reserved.

Portions of chapter 8 in the section "Engaging the culture, sort of" are adapted from "Seattle Pacific University: The College of Choice for Earnest Young Rockers with $90,000 and No Sex Drive Whatsoever," *The Stranger*, September 25, 2003. Online: http://www .thestranger.com/seattle/Content?oid=15771. All rights reserved.

Portions of chapter 10 are adapted from "MP3 Porn: Music, Sex, and Community," *The Other Journal* no. 7 (June 13, 2006). Online: http:// www.theotherjournal.com/article.php?id=152. All rights reserved.

Portions of chapter 11 in the section "The Absolutely True Story of My Failed Attempt to Join a Chinese Death Metal Band" are adapted from "Joining the Chinese Heavy Metal Band," Good Letters: The *Image* Blog, March 5, 2010. Online: http://imagejournal.org/page/ blog/joining-the-chinese-heavy-metal-band. All rights reserved.

Portions of chapter 12 in the section "And You Give Yourself Away" are adapted from "The End of Musical Memory," Good Letters: The *Image* Blog, October 22, 2009. Online: http://imagejournal.org/ page/blog/the-end-of-musical-memory. Also portions in the section "What I Write about When I Write about Music and Religion" are adapted from "What I Write about When I Write about Music and Religion," Good Letters: The *Image* Blog, January 22, 2009. Online: http://imagejournal.org/page/blog/what-i-write-about-when-i-write-about-music-and-religion. All rights reserved.

Introduction

The Un-Scene: A Confession

A little throat clearing, before I step up to the microphone. I have to be honest: as much as I have always wanted to write this book, I kind of do not want to write this book.

For years, I tried not to write it. I tried fiction, but gave up after an instructor couldn't get me to fix the ending to the story where a seventeen-year-old kid loses his virginity in the freezer at a convenience store. I tried "music journalism," writing stories nobody read about bands I didn't care about for a tiny newspaper that hardly paid me anything. I got a couple of college degrees. I did fund-raising and filing for some nonprofit organizations. I moved to California, China, and Canada. I went back to school *again*. No matter what I do, though, I can't escape the fact that popular music and Christianity have made me who I am, and whatever else I try to write, those two themes elbow everything else out of the way, growing more persistent, so that every time I sit down at the computer, that is all that comes out.

I started writing about Christian rock in my parents' basement at age fifteen; a self-never-published zine called *Toxic Chalk*[1] ran for four issues as a ClarisWorks document on my dad's computer. The compulsion to understand the three-way relationship between music and faith and me has been on my mind since at least the time I heard

---

1. Years later, someone pointed out the unfortunate similarities between this name and a rare medical syndrome associated with tampon use. Perhaps it's for the best that I never published my zine.

1

"The Hardway" by dc Talk and "Jesus He Knows Me" by Genesis, and I'm out of excuses. I have too much of the sticky residue of pop radio and Christian bookstores, of punk rock and youth group, of Catholic school and garage bands, and of Christian college and smoky rock bars stuck to my soul not to do this.

So on with the show, but before that (because shows always start way, way later than they should), let's get something out of the way: you are reading a book about listening to music. Reading is just sitting and looking at words somebody made up, and listening doesn't even require looking—you can sit motionless, with your eyes closed, in a dark room, and do it. Surely there is no more passive activity than reading a book about listening to music, because what is going to happen? Will there be a *story*? *Can* there be a story?

See, in school, when they teach you about how to write what is called "creative nonfiction," you hear a lot of talk about "scenes." Every piece of writing consists of scenes, short, snappy little retellings of compelling events, so that the action moves along and readers are drawn in by the real details of the story. The idea is that people don't want to sit reading page after page about *what somebody thinks*. Without scenes, nothing happens. After reading hundreds of pages of ideas, thoughts, and feelings, it's easy to respond like the Dude in *The Big Lebowski*: "Well, that's just, like, your *opinion*, man." We want scenes, real things that happened to real people who have led lives more interesting than ours. We want to know what they have done, and how, and why.

What I have done, mostly, is listen to music. And one of the things about listening to music is that on the surface there are no stories, no scenes. Or if there are scenes, they are all the same. Take this timeline, for example:

1984:   I am sitting on a beanbag chair between two Bose speakers listening to a gospel record.

1990:   I am sitting in my bedroom, a cassette poised on record/pause, waiting to hear the new Boyz II Men single.

1995:   I am standing in a church basement listening to Sixpence None the Richer play.

1998:   I am standing in a theater in downtown Spokane listening to Built to Spill play.

2001:   I am standing at the Showbox in downtown Seattle listening to Death Cab for Cutie play.

2009:   I am sitting in front of a computer wearing a pair of Sennheiser headphones and listening to a song by an obscure '90s Christian grunge band.[2]

These are not scenes; they are un-scenes. They are the picture of passivity—there is just music, just noise traveling through the air, past the cochlea, into the brain. Nothing to see here, folks. Every significant musical moment looks the same, and on the surface it is the same, because what is essential in the music scene, the personal action and reaction you get from music, is hidden.

But in this unseen un-scene,[3] there is something more unwieldy than a scene, something that spins out of control, that lends itself to skips and jumps in consciousness—songs remind us of things that happened, things that happened remind us of songs, songs remind us of songs, and in the course of a three-minute guitar ditty we have traveled the entire world without moving. Cue up "Hell" by the Squirrel Nut Zippers, and while we are grooving to the pseudocalypso, I will be thinking about the girl who bought me the *first* Squirrel Nut Zippers record for my seventeenth birthday, even though she knew I already owned it, and wondering what possessed her to do that and where she is now. I'll think of the first time I saw the music video and the argument I had with my best friend about whether or not the girl singer was a man—she wasn't—and I'll think about what exactly hell is, and whether or not it is something I should be worried about, and whether the guy who wrote the song was being jokey or a little serious about the fire-and-brimstone, or if it's just a convention of the genre refracted through postmodern '90s irony. Songs move, and they move *us*, so quickly and in such mysterious and personal ways.

If this book moves, I hope it moves in the way pop songs do. There will be a lot of talk about songs, but inasmuch as this is a book about listening to music, it's also about how listening to music makes us who we are, or at least about how it makes me who I am, and so it is an exploration, an idiosyncratic and opinionated and particular one, of a self shaped by the oddly intersecting forces of

2. "Bliss Is" by Poor Old Lu.

3. I promise to stop doing this.

the American evangelical Protestant church and the American popular music scene. I don't mean for that to sound hoity-toity—if this were fifteen years ago, I would say that this book was about Christian music, and I would know exactly what I meant. My purpose now is not only to talk about "Christian music." I am not here to explicate Christian music, to explain why it exists and whether it is any good.[4] Instead, think of what you're about to read as like an iPod playlist, a collection of essays and thoughts on listening to music and having faith and how they have made me, and a lot of people like me, and maybe you.

Also, there will be some jokes about Stryper.

I used to be a lot angrier about the relationship between pop music and Christianity. I was planning to write a book called *The Death of Christian Rock*, which would have been a lot more dramatic and sexy and controversial. Also, nobody would have read it, because the intended audience—people who listen to Christian music—would have hated it. Still, to proclaim the death of Christian pop music, to celebrate it and dance on its grave and wish it an unpleasant afterlife, was once an imperative for me. I wanted to tell everybody that Christian music is a terrible idea and that nobody should ever listen to it and that it gives you a lot of weird ideas that make it hard to be a normal, well-adjusted adult person.[5] I wanted to explain that the only true musical salvation will come from super-indie DIY ethics, that it was all an ideological and economic problem, and that if you throw away your MercyMe and Creed CDs and start your own zine and book your own all-ages venue and only buy CDs at independent record stores, you'll be Doing the Right Thing.

But something weird happened to me while I was writing: I started listening to Christian music again. In the middle of my anti-Christian-music screed, I suddenly noticed that almost every record I was listening to for work (I occasionally get paid, though not very

4. No.

5. This is a huge exaggeration, but it *is* mind-blowing to be running in the same pack as people who write rock & roll songs about how evolution is wrong. See Geoff Moore & the Distance.

much, to write about music), and most of the records I was listening to for fun, had something in common: they were all *way, way* religious, more so even than the music I used to love when I was a Christian rock fan. *The Death of Christian Rock* started to look like a dishonest book—did I really want to make some well-meaning kid quit his youth group praise band? Because if I had done that, I would not have learned how to play and love music the way I did when I was younger. Did I want to tell people to stop buying Christian magazines that tell them what bands they ought to be listening to? Because those magazines sometimes pay me to do that very thing. Did I really want to risk the anonymous online wrath of some righteous fundamentalist who felt offended by my mocking of praise & worship music? Because, after all, my main goal as a writer is to not have my feelings hurt by readers who disagree with me.

I decided to change tactics. The new plan was a manifesto about everything that could be *right* about the relationship between pop music and Christianity—I was going to find the bands ("Christian" or not) that have done and are doing music worth listening to for people who care about faith and music. There are plenty of them, and I've been building a modest mini-career writing about them for the last ten years. I toned down my cynicism and finger-pointing, no longer berating people for listening to the Newsboys instead of the Smiths or making it my mission to explain why '90s U2 is actually more spiritually significant than '80s U2.

When I told an editor at *Christianity Today* that I wanted to write a new "Christian music listener" manifesto,[6] he wasn't enthused. "I'm not interested in any articles on 'Why You Aren't Listening to Music Correctly,'" he said. Fair enough: I would focus on providing gentle, nonjudgmental suggestions about the wonderful music you *could* be listening to. I would avoid telling young bands what to do, although my spider-sense wants very much to tell any band considering signing with a Christian record label to run very quickly in the opposite direction and not to stop running until reaching the nearest indie record store or all-ages nonprofit venue.

That book, too, died rather quickly, because it was also an unnecessary crusade. It didn't make sense to prod, however gently, David

6. That's "*Christian* music listener," not "*Christian music* listener."

Crowder fans to start listening to Sleater-Kinney, because *I* don't even listen to Sleater-Kinney,[7] and people are not wrong to prefer certain kinds of music to others. I wanted to make a case that boozy Canadian indie rock bands are somehow a powerful force for the gospel. I wanted to surprise Joe Agnostic Rock Dude (who listens to the Shins, reads his local alt weekly, drinks microbrews at the downtown rock venue, sleeps in late and does the crossword on Sundays[8]) into seeing his music in a new way. But I don't think he'd care, and he wouldn't know enough about the Prayer Chain or Amy Grant to want to read the parts about them. And if I were too gentle, I'd never persuade the people who might need to hear it: the crazy anti-Christian-rock zealots on the Internet, who damn everyone from Amy Grant to P.O.D. to hell over accusations of satanism. There was no argument here, no reformation. The manifesto was not a manifesto at all.

If you grew up evangelical, especially if you grew up "nondenominational," it can be hard to find a grand narrative to describe your experience, because evangelicals are big on just doing whatever. Or, rather, we like to feel like we're just doing whatever, like we are free and easy and we're doing this Jesus thing in a natural, normal way, and we don't have rituals or costumes or bells and whistles. In fact, we do have our rules and our social codes; one is that we are not a tribe who take easily to creeds or manifestos. Some people—mostly reporters who visit famous megachurches to report on the inscrutable natives with all the nuance and grace of nineteenth-century anthropology—think we follow rules blindly. But many evangelicals would tell you otherwise. We are, in fact, encouraged to create our own stories rather than submitting to hierarchies—we resist grand histories, and we go looking for roots in weird places. Where I have found mine is in music played with guitars and drums.

Like most thirtyish Christian rock fans,[9] people who are immersed in the worlds of faith and popular culture, I have had my

7. "All Hands on the Bad One" is an awesome song, though.

8. All of this describes me, too, by the way, but the difference is that I feel guilty about not going to church while I'm doing the crossword.

9. And here I mean both *Christian rock* fans and Christian *rock fans*.

conversions and deconversions and reconversions. They have been not only religious, but cultural and ideological. I know that I am a confused person with great love for mysteries of faith and music. I know that I am wired for Christianity and I am wired for popular music, and the stuff that most moves me, that has really taken over my life, is the stuff that blends the two. I know that I only understand these things when I write about them. I know that what I am is somebody who cannot escape God or guitars.

And that is why this isn't an angry rant or a manifesto, and I am not here to convince anybody about anything. Honestly, what has emerged is a kind of simultaneous deconstruction and celebration of faith and music. And what keeps me from being embarrassed about how self-centered this is is remembering how relatively unremarkable such a life is for people of my generation and background.

I remember reading a news story once about some students at a Christian college who were angry that the Pledge of Allegiance had been discontinued at a certain campus event. One student said that to him, taking away the pledge was like removing a part of his faith, that there was no separation between his religious belief and his patriotism. I was quick to point the finger and make simulated vomiting noises, but I'm beginning to see how I am that guy, how I have done the same with music, how difficult it has been for me to separate the movement of spirit from the movement of melody and guitar solo. For me—and for a lot of people—rock is almost part of my religion itself, or at least it's mixed up with my religion, and I see little chance of extricating it. Being a twenty-first-century, postmodern evangelical Christian with an unhealthy obsession for rock & roll bands is the story I find myself in.

All right, let's go. 1–2, 1–2, is this thing on?

By the way, each of these chapters concludes with a list of five records mentioned, or at least implicated, during that chapter. These could be considered "reviews," but I prefer to think of them as recommendations—I really do recommend almost every record mentioned in the forthcoming pages, including and maybe even especially the ones I make fun of, and I think you should buy them. You'll probably find most of them in a Used/Rejected/Irrelevant/Uncool bin at your local record store. But you know, that's where all the best records usually are anyway.

1

In the Beginning

RECORDS

Like most men my age who were never very good at PE, I love records. I don't mean *vinyl* records. I find those kind of annoying and a
lot less portable than an iPod, unless you are one of the guys I went
to college with who always wore messenger bags shaped exactly like
a record so that everyone knew they were purists on their way to
the record store to buy a limited edition seven-inch on red vinyl.
Honestly, those big round things my parents used to listen to are not
even a meaningful part of reality now (though I did go through an
expensive phase with them).

When I say "records," I mean "albums," which could mean LPs,
cassettes, CDs, or even just files on a computer. *Record* is a versatile
word—it's what your grandparents listened to on those old-fangled
Victrolas, it's what the Beatles made, it's what you can make with your
friends in the basement with a computer and some microphones. A
record does not even have to be encoded on a physical object. In fact,
record doesn't even have to mean an album; the National Academy of
Recording Arts & Sciences has a Grammy award called "Record of the
Year," which is awarded for a song.

But there is another meaning for *record* that makes all the difference, because *to make a record* is to capture, for a time, how things are—

to preserve for posterity a time and a place and a feeling. Photographs, diaries, and newspapers can be records. And records can be records.

The first record, for me, the one I remember seeing actually spin around on a turntable, is *Great Moments in Gospel Music*, which was a thank-you gift that the Christian aid organization World Vision mailed to donors, including my parents. The title of this record is ironic, because the music on it is not, in fact, gospel music in the high-energy black-church sense. Encoded in its grooves is something called CCM or Contemporary Christian Music, which is something like "adult contemporary" music that is marketed only to evangelical Christians, is vaguely inspirational, occasionally refers to God, and is sung by earnest men and women with outdated haircuts. I didn't like all the songs on the record, and my mom always turned it off before the Sandi Patty song, because even though she had been a Christian for almost ten years, there were some things my mother wasn't willing to put up with. My favorite songs on the record were "The Warrior Is a Child" by Twila Paris,[1] "Angels" by Amy Grant, and "Great Is the Lord" by Michael W. Smith.

I don't care about your musical or religious proclivities—"Great Is the Lord" is a damn good song. It's part hymn, part symphony–operatic choral epic, part progressive rock, part evangelical praise chorus. Its mix of classical styles, '80s synthesizers, and guitar solos is pitch-perfect, and the song builds to a frenzy, with the chorus modulating higher and higher till the very last repetition of the title, which features one of the most pregnant pauses ever recorded in a Christian pop song, followed by a terrifying "LOOOOOOOOOORD!" The choir hits an impossibly high note,[2] holding it for measures over the progged-out, syncopated drum and guitar hits, finally melting into a mixture of pipe organ and guitar feedback that rings out, echoing in endless triumph.

That recording was so inspiring, rocked so hard, that I told my parents I wanted to write a song (I must've been about five), so my

1. I find that I still have a soft spot for this song, though I cannot imagine what made me identify with the "warrior" part, nor can I imagine how Twila Paris managed to convincingly represent herself as one.

2. Interestingly enough, this interval, this sudden jump into a heavenly octave on "Lord," is almost identical to the one Sufjan Stevens uses twenty years later on "Seven Swans."

father, a music teacher, played the piano while I sang the words I'd made up. The words are lost now, but they were nearly an exact duplicate of "Great Is the Lord" except that the lyrics were in a different order. We later performed this song at my parents' evangelical church, no doubt to the *oohs* and *aahs* of the congregation.

I do not remember very much about being five years old, and most of what I do remember is because there are photographs. I remember that there was a horse someplace near our house and that I had a kite with Snoopy and Woodstock on it, but beyond that, things get a little sketchy. One thing I am sure of is that I was not trying to be cute when I wrote that song. I think I was trying to be awesome, responding to the awesomeness of a piece of music I had heard, which was, in turn, Michael W. Smith responding to the awesomeness he found in God. It remains only one of a handful of songs that have come from my brain. A lot has changed since then, obviously—that was twenty-five years ago—but the deeper one looks into one's past, the less one seems to have changed. The things that matter to me most—God and rocking out, words and music, faith and songs—are things I learned from *Great Moments in Gospel Music*, which sits on a shelf above my desk now, although I don't own a record player.

Having this piece of plastic, a tangible piece of personal, musical, cultural, and religious history, in my possession makes me wonder how a world came to exist in which I still hang on to this record, how the building blocks of my passion for music came together even before my birth. I have done a lot of reading about the evangelical pop subculture to try to figure out whether or not I am crazy and to see what people, Christian or not, have to say about it. One thing I have noticed is this: if the writer is a Christian, the story of Christian rock music is a story of people breaking free from conventions in order to express their worship of God in the way that moves them most; it is the best possible marriage of God's spirit and people's modern-day creativity. If a non-Christian, or even a non-evangelical, is writing, they mostly speak about how Christian music is a calculated and sinister marketing ploy, designed to trick naive teenagers into accepting a harmful, fundamentalist belief system, and about how the music is inevitably tied up with ultra-conservative political causes. I suspect the real story is both or neither.

The farther away I get from what people like me refer to as my "Christian rock days," the more I am confused about what was going on, why the music was so important to me, and why it still seems to have a hold on my imagination even though I don't buy tobyMac records. Why should it matter much, now, that for about four or five years in the '90s I was really into Christian rock music? A while ago I got a response when I posed a similar question in something I wrote on the Internet. One reader answered with a clarity I had never been able to articulate: "Evangelical rock music is evangelical identity music."

And maybe that's it. To me, Christian rock was never a struggle to show that Christianity was "relevant" and "cool," nor did I feel sucked into a covert agenda to get me to vote Republican. Nor was it a magical "new" way to express faith in God, a Jesus Movement, hippie-style breaking with convention giving me the freedom to rock out with my faith out.[3] It also was not a way to proselytize (though I dragged a few non-Christian friends to shows with me out of a vague sense of duty) or to promote exclusive claims. Evangelical rock music is evangelical identity music, and so, Christian rock was me.

Of course, it was also many other things—a mash-up of seemingly disparate cultures, a passionate expression of belief through a commercial art form of the times that we were all really digging, and a weird little society very few people outside of the evangelical world had heard of. But at its core, Christian rock was something that *made* me, and it is not an easy thing to trace the pre-history that helped construct oneself.

What was the trajectory that led to my rocking out to a praise & worship song in Belgrade, Montana, in the early '80s, and then to my soul being destroyed and rebuilt at a punk rock show in a church basement in Spokane, Washington, in the '90s, and then to a turn-of-the-century life in Seattle writing record reviews on borrowed computers and playing psychedelic jams in church sanctuaries?

I don't know. I am not good at regular history,[4] but I have absorbed enough amateur music history to tell me something about

3. I will be making jokes like this all the way through. Sorry.

4. The only thing I remember from U.S. history, for example, is the way our teacher warned us that if the Russians attacked, we'd be the first target due to our close proximity to an Air Force base. This was in 1998.

how Christian rock came to be created and about how I ended up in the right place to get to it. So without further ado, I give you:

CHRISTIAN ROCK: AN INCOMPLETE, PARTIAL, BIASED, AND PRETTY MUCH ACCURATE HISTORY

What is Christian rock music and why does it exist? The best I can do is to say that Christian rock is rock music that is (probably but not necessarily) made by people who identify themselves as Christians and that is (probably but not necessarily) listened to by people who identify themselves as Christians. It gets murkier when we try to define Christian (and rock), because if we cast a wide and charitable net to catch those who claim that label, we will find a big percentage of people who aren't actually involved with Christian rock at all. CCM is largely an evangelical phenomenon, not a mainline Protestant or Catholic or Mormon one, which means we are limited to about 25 percent of the U.S. population. And not all of *those* people listen to it, because I am one and I don't. The point is, it's a small demographic, but a big-ish cultural phenomenon.

There are a few other books that can give you a picture of the history of Christian music,[5] but the story basically goes like this: rock & roll (which was created possibly by Bill Haley and the Comets, maybe by Elvis, probably by the Beatles) is conceived, born, and begins to mature sometime between 1950 and 1960. At some point, rock bands stop being polite young men in matching suits and become drug-addled, free-loving, infrequent-bath-taking hippies, and the music gets more interesting. The hippies later realize that taking tons of acid has not actually made their lives quantifiably better, and they become disillusioned; some of them become lawyers, but some find Christianity to be a more satisfying alternative, establishing a kind of counter-counterculture called the Jesus Movement. These people (also called Jesus Freaks) are still hippies, but with less drugs and sex and more Jesus. More Jesus, in fact, than a lot of churches, who (the Jesus Freaks think) are focused too much on rules and rituals and not enough on the joy of the Lord. Converts though they are, these emerging Jesus rockers are not keen on stodgy church music (it's part

5. You should still buy this one, though.

of the problem), and so they keep playing rock & roll, but—and this is key—they do not go back to the politeness and the matching suits. They keep their beards and torn jeans, and the Jesus Freaks start touring churches with their bands. Other Christians start to realize that (a) these people seem legit, faithwise, and (b) kids seem to like this kind of music.

This is where you should put down this book and ask someone who was alive before 1980, but somehow a collusion of churches, businessmen, parachurch organizations, rock bands, and musicians gets together and establishes some Christian record labels. These labels are fairly small and independent, but in the '80s a lot of people start buying records from them, the economic gears get moving, and soon something large enough to be called a "Christian music industry" exists—both in a "mainstream" or wholesome, money-making, and authority-approved form and in an "underground" or youth-oriented, not particularly money-making, and suspiciously authority-unfriendly form.[6]

By the beginning of the 1990s, Christian music of all genres and proclivities is beginning to melt into one glorious spectacle of noise, faith, money, and culture—all lines are blurred save the one that separates "Christian" from "secular." You start to see Christian records (but not many) in regular record stores, and Christian bookstores, which once sold only Bibles and cross necklaces, stocking Christian heavy metal and gangsta rap albums. There are Christian fake-indie labels pouring money into records by great bands, Christian indie labels with no money putting out bad records, and vice versa. Grunge rebel songs and ballads about chastity are played one after the other on Christian radio. Metrosexual Christian pop singers open shows for nu-metal Christian rock bands. Everyone is buying records, and Christian bands fight their way to the upper third of the Billboard charts. This lasts for most of the decade, until the turn of the century, when everyone stops buying CDs, the Christian indie rock bands get fed up with the profit-driven audience-pandering (sometimes referred to as the "Jesus Per Minute" rule) and pull up stakes to try their luck

6. A lot of people would disagree, I guess, that Christian music can ever be "authority-unfriendly," but those people do not realize that the Man is not always who you think it is.

in "the world," and the Christian industry consolidates itself, musically, by focusing on artists who sound like Coldplay and U2: epic E-bowed guitars, soaring choruses, and lyrics—loud in the mix—about wonder and worship.

This, I assume, is where we are now, although I stopped listening to Christian music just after what I will now ostentatiously refer to as its Golden Age (roughly 1993–2000)—which just happens to coincide with my own adolescence—when people like me realized that God, or at least traces and hints of him, was all over the place and that there was much more of him to be found outside the confines of the Christian bookstore. And most everybody who made up the orbit of Christian rock and pop in the '90s—the writers, publications, musicians, labels, publicists, and venues—seem to have moved right along, too. You'd be hard-pressed to find a Christian music magazine or Web site started in the mid-'90s that still exists now,[7] and only the biggest and most financially robust record labels have survived. A few of the behind-the-scenes figures remain, but most of the writers whose names you used to see in *CCM Magazine* have either moved on to writing for *Paste* or jettisoned Christianity all together and built creative lives from the rubble.

A Christian music industry still exists, but it no longer resembles the vibrant scene it did in the '80s and '90s. The reason Christian music finally imploded may be, simply, that it does not have a definition. "Christian music" cannot really be defined by lyrical content, musical genre, or even the beliefs of the artist if you consider a hardcore band like Zao, whose rotating cast of members has included outspoken atheists, or a vocal group like Phillips, Craig & Dean, who are, depending on who you ask, heretics because their churches embrace "Oneness" theology, which rejects the traditional understanding of the Trinity.

What else is there? CCM, it seems, can only be recognized by virtue of its being marketed to Christians. All of those involved in the industry know what to expect: an artist is Christian if they are played on Christian radio, signed to a Christian record label, or sold in a Christian store. The problem with this setup is that no one has clearly defined what makes each of these facets of the Christian industry

---

7. RIP the *Lighthouse*, *7ball*, *Release*, *True Tunes News*, and NetCentral.

exclusively "Christian." The distressing answer may be that Christians are the people from whom they're making their money.

How did this unholy mess get rolling? Rock & roll is supposed to be the rebellion, and Christianity the establishment, and these assumptions have led many a lazy rock critic to write reviews and essays about Christian rock in which the thesis is, essentially, "Bwuh?!" The problem is, of course, that the rebellion and the establishment are never so well defined. Look at Larry Norman, whose 1969 debut album is sometimes called the first Christian rock record. Norman was a Jesus hippie, and neither the Christian establishment nor the music industry really knew what to do with him. His first record with the band People! was originally titled *We Need a Whole Lot More of Jesus, and a Whole Lot Less of Rock & Roll*. The record company retitled the album *Love* and the band fell apart. Norman went on to make solo records for decades, none of them particularly successful, but when he passed away in 2008 he was widely eulogized as the Father of Christian Rock. At the time of his death, Norman was working on an album with Frank Black of the Pixies and Isaac Brock of Modest Mouse. This certainly suggests that his influence was wide, but more importantly, if this album is ever released, the world will explode because it will be so weird and awesome.

Larry Norman may have been a pioneer for Christian rock in the born-again, "Bible-believing" sense,[8] but a band called the Electric Prunes once claimed to have made the first Christian rock album. This is a much more complicated assertion than it seems, though: *Mass in F Minor* (the album in question) is indeed an old rock record, and based as it is on, um, the Mass, it seems to fit the criteria. But it all depends on what you mean by Christian, what you mean by rock, and what you mean by Christian rock. Aside from the contention that Christian rock should be made by people who are blatantly identifiable as card-carrying "I Used to Take Horse Tranquilizers but the Lord Saved Me" evangelical Christians,[9] which the Prunes don't seem to fit, a lot of people don't agree that *Mass in F Minor* was even the first. There are other candidates that get thrown around, bands

---

8. This is code meaning "Only we are right about the Bible."

9. I cannot find the original citation for this, so I will not mention the prominent Christian singer whose testimony included a horse tranquilizer addiction.

I know very little about, like Love Song, Peter R. Scholtes, the Holy Smoke Doo Dah Band, or the Joystrings. In the liner notes to a reissue of the album, though, the claim is made by one of the Prunes that *Mass in F Minor* is the first Christian rock album.

That was 1967. By a rough estimate, rock & roll was invented in about 1955, and this puts the Prunes album pretty early in rock history, meaning that, for as long as there has been rock, there has been Christian rock. I had to wait most of my life for people like Sufjan Stevens to come along and show that popular music influenced by the Christian faith didn't have to be motivated by money or keeping up appearances or following mainstream trends in order to win converts—all of which are sins that "Christian music" as an industry has been guilty of at one time or another—but it's comforting to know that there were people mingling Jesus with rock & roll before I was even born, and not just the Prunes. Other obscure '60s and '70s artists like Judee Sill, Silmaril, the Trees Community, and many other bands you've never heard of[10] made compelling pop/rock music with an undeniably Christian bent even before Christian record labels existed.

Really, my concept of "Christian music," which begins in about 1980 and ends in 2000 (around the time I got bored with it), is nothing but a snapshot. It ignores decades of gospel, country, blues, and folk music, not to mention centuries of classical and early music. These are musical traditions in which it was unusual *not* to sing about God. The conventional line about Christianity and (rock) music being a contradiction in terms is about as inaccurate as a positive review of a Creed album. It's music *without* God that is, historically, an anomaly. Perhaps the Christian pop I grew up with was simply reparation for a weird gap in time when, for some reason, music *wasn't* being made for the glory of God. Whatever the reason, I was born in the thick of a Christian rock explosion, and from the time I first dropped the needle on *Great Moments in Gospel Music*, my fate was sealed: these were the kind of records that were going to define me.

10. I have to thank Thom Jurek and others at Artsandfaith.com for turning me on to many of these strange and wonderful Christian bands of the '60s and '70s.

FIVE ALBUMS FROM THE MURKY PRE-HISTORY OF CHRISTIAN ROCK

Amy Grant, *The Collection* (1986, Myrrh/A&M)

A brief topography of Amy Grant scandals: mainstream record label. Bare feet. "Sexy" videos. Divorce. Vince Gill. Amy Grant's first greatest hits album was released while she was still teetering between CCM and what those in the Christian record biz call the "general market," a term that is so embarrassing to use outside of Christian music circles, an admission that CCM is a tiny, self-imposed ghetto. *The Collection* was released in 1986, when Amy Grant was still young and not divorced and was CCM's first best pop star. It's a great group of songs, and Michael W. Smith plays three kinds of synthesizers on it, which could not possibly be a bad thing. There's a lovely combination of worship songs and vaguely "secular" songs, often in the form of romantic advice to friends, which makes this collection of early Amy Grant material a refreshingly realistic look at evangelical Christian life—how tied up in (messy) human relationships it is. From the outside, it may look like evangelicalism is all straight-up, over-spiritual praise like "Thy Word" and "El Shaddai," but it's also the simple friendship of "Stay for a While" and the steadfast devotion of "Love Can Do."

The Electric Prunes, *Release of an Oath* (1968, Reprise)

By the time they got to the less-celebrated (but superior) *Release of an Oath*, the Electric Prunes no longer existed—David Axelrod, the idiosyncratic Jewish composer/producer who wrote *Mass in F Minor*, had been, for some years, in the process of making the Electric Prunes moniker his own, and this record is almost entirely his doing. That it comes from a more obscure (by Christian standards) Jewish liturgy stands out as a dramatic statement. The lyrics are quite beautiful and cutting, lamenting oaths made under duress and unkept promises to God. After the singing, Axelrod leaves a lot of instrumental space (even some drum solos), and strings in particular carry a lot of weight, but the melodies are so memorable that they feel lyrical. The instrumental hook in "Holy Are You" clearly echoes its lyrics—mostly a repetition of the song's title—and it's reminiscent of the three-note mantra in John Coltrane's *A Love Supreme*, the instrumental representation of the words "Thank You, God."

Judee Sill, *Heart Food* (1973, Asylum)

Judee Sill's life was short and sad, and her musical career remains tragically underappreciated. A folksinger with a heart for the holy and a hankering for heroin, her second album is a masterpiece, from the gospelly "There's a Rugged Road" to the baroque epic "The Donor," which Sill once said was written to "musically induce God into giving us all a break." That "The Donor" is the longest song Sill recorded doesn't automatically make it her best—"The Kiss" accomplishes astral-plane-takeoff in under three minutes and with vast simplicity. It's just that Sill's vision, her feeling, the gravitas of her work is embodied in "The Donor," a recognition of the unhappy human condition while yearning for communion. It starts with a slow and plodding piano riff, just one note after another. Then you begin to notice other instruments—tympani in the background, Sill's multitracked vocals humming a melody. A vibraphone adds a countermelody, another layer of Sill's vocals start singing "Kyrie" (have mercy), and next other voices are added that also sing "Kyrie." This builds to a climactic chorus of "Kyrie Elaison" (Lord, have mercy), a huddled mass of humanity united, pleading for mercy. If this isn't reason enough to give Judee Sill a listen, my other favorite thing about her is that she was an Amy Grant fan.

The Trees Community, *Christ Tree* (1975, Hand/Eye)

I guess this record isn't "pop." It's more like folk meets choral music meets Christian rock meets Indian ragas meets renaissance festivals meets hippies meets poetry meets liturgy. Kinda. The Trees were an intentional Christian community in New York in the '70s and, like a number of other fringy Christian groups whose recordings have been rediscovered by crate diggers in recent years, they made a great album that almost nobody heard until it was reissued in the 2000s. *Christ Tree* is strange and beautiful. There's a sense of joyous freedom throughout the collection (the CD rerelease includes four discs of music, collecting one original LP with demos and live performances), incorporating Middle Eastern drones, ecclesiastical chant, percussion breakdowns, hymns, a cappella choir numbers, shouting, and chaotic jams. "Jesus He Knows" is as gentle and soothing as "Elijah" is freaky and jarring. The Trees Community could be called a forerunner of a band like the Polyphonic Spree, but I get the feeling that where the Spree fabricated their cultish schtick, the Trees were dead serious about their devotion to God and community.

 Peter R. Scholtes, *They'll Know We Are Christians by Our Love* (1968, FEL)

The Catholic Church has never had quite such a cozy relationship with rock music as the Evangelical Kingdom of America has had. This is not really a bad thing, until you see Catholics try to get "contemporary" with music. The few contemporary-style Catholic services I have been to tended to feature a man with a beard or a woman with a short, severe haircut playing an acoustic guitar, usually worn at an absurdly high position on the torso. If you have been to a more rocking Mass, feel free to disagree. There was, in fact, a tradition of "folk masses" started in the mid-twentieth century. Peter R Scholtes, in the 1960s, was a Catholic priest (he wrote the title track), and the recordings he made are quite possibly the first attempts at Catholic rock; he did a bossa nova version of the Mass, which grooves, if not exactly like a Getz/Gilberto recording, at least like a liturgical, Up with People-y, the Mamas & the Papas sort of thing. It's pretty good, and avoids drifting into untethered, feel-good, happy-clappy Protestant territory, possibly because some of the musicians were teenage gang members from Chicago.

2

Rock & Roll to Please Your Soul

AT THE ZOO

Christian radio stations like to market themselves as "family-friend-ly." Before the commercials, you'll hear those little ads for the sta-tions themselves, which feature listeners calling in and saying things like "It's just so nice to have a radio station the whole family can listen to in the car," or "I'm glad I've found a station I don't have to worry about my kids listening to," or "Thanks, 104.5 KJZS-FM, for the positive, uplifting, nonthreatening, bland, humorless, white-bread, boring simulacra of pop music you play so I don't have to think." I exaggerate slightly, but a lot of people seem to want their pop music without the risk of hearing swear words or blatant sexual come-ons. Some turn to Christian radio; the rest of us turn to oldies.

Oldies was what my mom listened to in the car a lot, so it was what I listened to, and the music was, as far as I was concerned, re-ally good.[1] The Beatles, the Monkees, Motown, girl groups—who can deny the great melodies and hooks?

1. What you do not realize when you are younger is that "oldies" refers not so much to the *songs* played on the station as it does to the *listeners*. It's not that they only play old songs, because the songs keep changing as the years go by. I note with some dread that the music on oldies stations is creeping past the mid-1970s now, which means they will soon arrive at music recorded during my lifetime. With any luck, by then radio will not exist, so we will not have to be reminded of our mortality and can continue blissfully listening to Animal Collective on our iPhones.

I would wait by the radio for Simon and Garfunkel songs to come on the oldies station so I could record them and learn the original versions—and some songs I'd never heard, like "Cecelia," which brazenly featured the singer "making love" (I was not certain what this entailed), and "At the Zoo" (innocent fun, although now I think the hamsters were doing drugs). What I did not know was that while this music was good, it was not at all cool.

I'd had intimations that I was somehow missing something by listening to oldies, like when my friend Tim got the Red Hot Chili Peppers' *Blood Sugar Sex Magik* at his eleventh birthday party. As I stood listening to the lyrics of the title song, I felt like I needed to say something to everybody, like I was the only one who realized the truth: "Uh, guys—these songs are about sex! We do not know what sex is![2] We should not be listening to this!"

The other thing I felt like I needed to say when "Give It Away" came on was "Holy crap, this song is awesome." Some people—crazy people, mostly—still argue that rock music is inherently sexual because of its rhythm, that the very name of the genre suggests intercourse, and that if kids listen to it, they'll start having orgies in the jungle. And while a lot of music *is* about sex—"Give it Away" certainly is—what you know when you're a kid is that it's a lot of fun. It wasn't the *Sex Magik* part that got me; it was Flea's bouncy, elastic bass lines, the twangy mouth harp that somehow transcended its redneck roots and became a funk groove, and that mind-bending backward guitar solo.

Cautiously, I started listening to the local Top 40 station, known as "93 Zoo FM," also known as "the Zoo," and for a period in the mid-'90s, "the All-New Zoo." I started hearing bands like C+C Music Factory, whose songs were mostly about fun, though Freedom Williams sounds *dead serious* about dancing on "Gonna Make You Sweat."[3] On another single, "Here We Go, Let's Rock & Roll," the chorus raises the stakes, saying that rock & roll can please your soul.

2. Well, I mean, we kind of did, because later that night while we were talking about girls, Tim dared a kid to stick his wiener in a glass of water and then drink it. But we certainly didn't know enough for songs about sex to be meaningful in any way.

3. Which is *not* actually called "Everybody Dance Now."

My dad heard me listening to this song in my bedroom once. "Rock & roll can please your soul?" he said. "What's that supposed to mean?"

"It's just music," I said.

My dad was and is not much of a pop music fan; he has been a music teacher for thirty years and listens mostly to jazz and classical. He acknowledges that the Beatles are good but says that his being made to listen to rock & roll is like a calculus professor being made to do his fours times tables. Also, it allows him to lord his fatherly knowledge over me, which I am looking forward to doing to my own future children, so I can't blame him for it. And it's not entirely his fault: he grew up in Montana, which is somewhere between ten and three hundred years behind the rest of the pop culture world.

"Well, don't listen to it," he said. "The lyrics are subliminal."

They didn't seem subliminal at all, but it was too late. I knew the secret: rock & roll—contemporary rock & roll, not rock from thirty years ago—really did please my soul. So between fourth and fifth grade, I switched allegiances from Oldies 101 to 93 Zoo FM.

Every city has two radio stations like this, and they are probably owned by the same national company. But that doesn't stop the musical difference, the difference in attitude and age, from being important to an eleven-year-old. Switching from Oldies 101[4] to the Zoo was nothing short of an identity change. I remember a short conversation I had with Tim, who was the trendiest kid in our class. He wore Stussy T-shirts and put gel in his spiked hair; I wore Goodwill T-shirts and parted my hair directly down the center.

"Joel, you're a lot cooler this year than you were last year," he explained. "You used to listen to Oldies and now you listen to the Zoo."

4. I want to pause here to acknowledge an audacious thing this station did. When my family first moved to Spokane, KEYF 101.1 was an easy listening station, playing the most heinous New Age music you have ever heard in your life. Instead of acknowledging that they were switching to an oldies format, the station suddenly, without warning, one day began playing nothing but "Louie, Louie" by the Kingsmen, arguably the greatest rock & roll song of all time. This continued for a week, and then two weeks. Then, different versions of "Louie, Louie" started to come—Richard Berry's original, one by Tina Turner, Paul Revere and the Raiders, a crazy Russian guy singing it, a Fat Boys rap version, dozens and dozens of covers. This continued for at least a month before the station switched to its oldies format. Frankly, it is the best thing a radio station has ever done.

If he were right, it was for one reason: I was no longer listening to the pop music my mom did. Intuitively, I knew I liked music, but I hadn't yet exercised my own judgment when it came to choosing what to listen to. This wasn't exclusive to oldies, either: before I made the switch to the Zoo, an older kid asked me who my favorite band was, and I told him it was the Manhattan Transfer. He punched me in the throat. I imagine this had less to do with his distaste for vocal jazz than the prepubescent pecking order, but nevertheless, things were different now: I was a loyal listener to the Zoo, and if I were going to get throat-punched, it wasn't going to be because I didn't know who Color Me Badd was.

It would be difficult for me to overestimate the amount of time I spent listening to the radio as a child, or even how much I listen to it now. A best guess, then as now, is all the time. The conservative talk station with my dad in the morning on the way to school;[5] oldies with mom on the way back home; the Zoo in my bedroom, cassette poised to record "I Can't Dance" by Genesis; AM sports talk to fall asleep. The radio was never not on, and today I cannot drive to the grocery store down the street without turning on NPR. Radio has always made me feel part of something bigger in an intimate, immediate way. There is comfort in knowing that I am not just alone in my bed listening to one person's voice, or one song, but that people like me and not like me all across the city or region or country are experiencing the same thing at the same time. Late at night, I sometimes tried to tune my radio to the in-between places on the dial, to see how far away I could travel through the signals. Sometimes I'd hear California stations, or Utah or Colorado. Radio was magic.

When we were in the second grade, my friend Daniel and I, while playing with walkie-talkies, believed we had made an important scientific discovery, because when we held the walkie-talkie antennae up to a metal pipe we could hear AM radio. "We should call the newspaper," I said. "They'll probably put our pictures on the front page," he said.[6] Radio, and the Zoo in particular, was like discovering a new world, an uncharted territory to be mapped.

5. Say what you will about Rush Limbaugh, but his radio program's theme song, "Ohio" by the Pretenders, is a great song.

6. They didn't.

FROM GENESIS TO CORINTHIANS

It was because of the radio that *We Can't Dance*, the fourteenth album by the British band Genesis, was technically the first pop album
(on cassette) I ever purchased with my own money, which is a *really
weird* choice for a fifth-grader to make when there were artists like
MC Hammer and Nirvana to pick from. Genesis is mostly irrelevant
to my generation; when I told my friend Zack about my new purchase, he exclaimed, "You got Genesis? Awesome! What games do
you have?" He was referring, of course, to the Sega Genesis, a home
video game system that came bundled with a menacing game called
Altered Beast,[7] which threatened to displace Nintendo's milquetoasty
Mario as the time waster of choice for preadolescent boys.

I'd played the Sega Genesis a few times at a neighbor's house, and
it was all right, but I'd heard "I Can't Dance" enough times on the
Zoo to know that I liked it and wanted to be able to listen to it at any
time of my choosing, and so on a family trip to Target I purchased *We
Can't Dance* for eleven dollars. The songs are not awful—in fact, "No
Son of Mine" and "Driving the Last Spike" could almost be sweeping
indie rock epics if they weren't sung by Phil Collins and bathed in
adult-contemporary synths—but they are hardly the epitome of the
Pop Year 1991.[8] I could maybe explain the purchase if it were 1984
and the record had been Genesis's self-titled album, or even 1986
when they released *Invisible Touch*, but *We Can't Dance?* A flaccid,
mid-career, easy-listening watercolor of an album?

I don't have an excuse. I just really liked the record. Plus, as
a tentative foray into the pop world, it seemed like a safe choice for
a sensitive Christian kid. *We Can't Dance* sat on my bedroom shelf
next to my Michael W. Smith *Go West Young Man* cassette (a birthday
gift from the previous year), an uneasy alliance in my young mind,
as I knew the Genesis record included an irreverent religious satire,
"Jesus He Knows Me." The song was dissing dishonest televangelists,
not Jesus himself, but still, I could not shake the feeling that there
was something wrong about listening to a band who flirted with

7. POWER UP.

8. That honor belongs to, of course, the following triumvirate of singles, the
quality of which the world has never known since: EMF's "Unbelievable," Jesus
Jones's "Right Here Right Now," and Big Audio Dynamite's "Rush."

blasphemy; also, one of the later tracks used the *if* word in describing God's existence, suggesting that the band members were, despite their biblical name, agnostic.

Then, after a few years of listening to the Zoo, of buying R & B Cassingles of Boyz II Men and Shai, of seeing Genesis and Smitty side by side on my shelf, I got the idea that I'd be better off listening to only Christian music. I had no sudden revelation, no spiritual "conviction" culminating in the burning of ungodly cassette tapes. And no one made me do it. When explaining how you got swept up in Christian music you are supposed to blame a repressive church, or your parents, or some kind of bizarre reverse peer pressure, yet my Sunday school teachers never showed us the classic anti-rock video *Hell's Bells*, in which a man with a mustache and a mullet explains the relationship between rock and satanism, and I *still* became convinced that secular rock music was at best a negative influence and at worst a debauched, demonic ritual. For some time I truly believed that secular rock concerts prominently featured live sex acts on stage.[9] Later, I learned that what they mostly feature is people looking bored and trying not to fall over drunk.

We were not, I should stress, fundamentalists. Sure, my parents subscribed to *Focus on the Family* magazine, and we sometimes went to church more than once a week, but there was also beer in the house, and we watched the *Simpsons*. This notion that secular rock music is really bad for you was, I think, a kind of leftover from the stricter fundie days of American evangelicalism, days in which drums and guitars were not yet possible paths to the Lord, but were invitations to sex, drugs, and ultimately, hell. By the 1980s and '90s, this anti-rock stance had softened into a simple formula: rock + God = good; rock − God = bad. But really, anything minus God equaled bad, and rock itself no longer had corrupting powers.

The badness of secular rock was simply something I came to understand, absorbing it in the atmosphere or through Sprite at youth group parties: Christian music is for Christians, and secular music

9. Obviously, this is crazy, but you also might want to read the interview with Marilyn Manson in the January 1997 *Rolling Stone* for at least one piece of evidence in my favor. I read this article while bored at a high school basketball game, and when I read Manson's explanations of his grotesquely sexed-up stage show, something deep in my subconscious evangelical mind went "Aha!"

is from "the world," and if there is one thing we are in and not of, it is the world. The Zoo was pretty clearly in the world, and I was a Christian and was old enough to make my own choices about music. Of course, my parents weren't disappointed by my decision—for one, they wouldn't have to worry about how my musical tastes might negatively influence my younger sister, who impressionably soaked up everything I did.[10] But all considerations of my family aside, I knew: it was time for me to start listening to CCM.

The conditions were ripe, and to transfer my fandom from Genesis and C+C Music Factory to dc Talk and PFR required only one gentle nudge: Christian rock radio. 101.9 FM was known as KTSL (K-The Salt and Light—really!) in Spokane, and for most of the week it played adult contemporary–style Christian hits, love songs with God in the role of boyfriend or girlfriend, or even that peculiar mutant hybrid of middle-aged singers warbling hymns over the top of Hall and Oates–style backing tracks (I am unaware of a name for this type of music). This was tolerable enough. It was a little dated, sure, but not much worse than the pop pabulum I had to sit through while waiting for the Zoo to play my favorite R & B singles. On Friday nights, however, the schlocky ballads gave way to a show that played some pretty badass rock and rap music. I say "badass" in remembering both my attitude about the music at the time (*this rocks, and I love it*) and reconsidering it many years later: it actually *was* creative and passionate and subversive compared to what passed for Christian culture at the time. For four hours every Friday, I took in song after song by PFR, Audio Adrenaline, dc Talk, the Newsboys, the Noisy Little Sunbeams,[11] Third Day, Sixpence None the Richer, Hoi Polloi, Poor Old Lu, Jars of Clay, the Prayer Chain, Dynamic Twins, and a host of gone-and-forgotten Christian bands whose music (just like C+C Music Factory had said!) did in fact please my soul. Not only could I be sure they were not performing any lewd acts on stage, but these were bands who seemed to have *me* in mind when they made music. This, finally, was it! This was music that did not compromise

10. As it turns out, though, she was more into show tunes anyway and is now a musical theater actor in New York.

11. Perpetrators of the truly horrific metal anthem "Turn or Burn," which condemns everyone from Madonna to Mormons to the pope to hell.

anything—it was not cryptically agnostic, it did not make me feel like I was cheating on my faith when I listened to it, and it was not selling twelve-year-old me sex and despair. But to only describe Christian rock in terms of what it was not would be unfair: it was also loud and exciting, weird and passionate, daring and hopeful. In fact, the music was sometimes *better*, not worse, than the stuff on the Zoo—the Friday night rock show could play a lot of weird stuff— hardcore punk and rap, say—when only bored Christian teenagers were listening, whereas the Zoo had to pander to the lowest common denominator[12] every day.

Friday after Friday, as I recorded these songs I was growing to love, I became sucked into their orbit by degrees, following the Christian rock path as far as it would take me, my knowledge and desire of this music spiraling toward more and more artists: I'd hear PFR on KTSL, buy their tape at Evangel Books and Gifts, and then pick up the *CCM* magazine as I left the store. In the magazine I'd read about a ton of other bands whose records I'd eventually buy, and I'd learn that PFR was on tour. I'd win tickets from KTSL to see PFR, and at the show I'd see bands like Hoi Polloi and Jars of Clay open for them, so I'd buy *their* records and go see *them* on their next tour, where I'd of course buy *their* opening band's records and T-shirts.

Obviously, this is how it works with any kind of music—ask a guy my age who's writing personal essays about his history with black metal, and he'll describe a similar cycle—but once I was immersed in the feedback loop of Christian music, it started to feel like a comfortable parallel universe, where we all read the same Book and all grooved to the same Cosmic DJ. The world was a scary place—too many subgenres of music to navigate, too many ideologies to choose from—so I stepped into a prefab mold, the Teenage Christian Rock Fan, which fit me just right. Within a few years, I was much more interested in Jars of Clay than anything Phil Collins was doing. I'd gone all the way from Genesis to 1 Corinthians 4:7, the Bible verse about "earthen vessels" from which Jars of Clay took their name.

12. Hence the popularity of Baltimora's "Tarzan Boy," which you may remember from a Listerine commercial at the time.

A DRAMATIC CONVERSION NARRATIVE INVOLVING A
SKA BAND

If you ask me to explain which Christian bands from the '90s I still like, I'll mention Sixpence None the Richer, Starflyer 59, and Danielson Famile. If you ask me to name some awesome, obscure Christian bands that quietly came and went, I'll go on and on about L. A. Symphony, the Prayer Chain, Luxury, Morella's Forest, and so on. But if you ask why I fell in love with Christian rock and pretty much had my life changed by it, I'll have a different answer.

A few years ago I heard a music critic, Jessica Hopper, give a talk on a favorite subject of music geeks: The Band That Saved My Life When I Was a Teenager (not the talk's actual title). To suggest that a rock & roll band could prevent someone from dying might seem melodramatic. It's preposterous to assume that teenagers can actually be aware of something as important as ideological salvation from the soul-killing *zeitgeist* when usually our biggest concerns are making it to that grocery-store bag-boy job by 3:30 or how that girl will never want to go to the prom with us. But we like to look back at our lives and create story arcs, and those of us who love music see it shaping our lives in profound ways, even from the beginning.

The band Hopper talked about was Bikini Kill. Bikini Kill shocked the young Ms. Hopper into something new. Bikini Kill blew up her grunge-and-boys world to the possibility of woman empowerment, girls in bands, zines, touring—and she grew up to be a great writer and critic because of it. After her talk (and an unsuccessful attempt to schmooze with her), I got to thinking: who was The Band for me? Who saved my life, that is, who helped to put me on a path toward something more profound, something I wouldn't have discovered otherwise?

The first rock band I truly, obsessively loved was the Minnesota trio PFR, a Christian rock band somewhere between the Beatles and Crowded House, whose pop songs I still think are exquisite. But I can't say they changed my life. Perhaps it was MxPx, then? A punk band from western Washington who sang about Jesus in one song and about anarchy and making out with chicks in another. Maybe, but then again, they were next to Green Day on the "If you like X evil secular band, you'll love Y Christian approximation of that band!" chart in the Christian bookstore, and I suspect *that* was the main thing I liked about MxPx. I can't even say that Sixpence None the Richer changed my life, even though I have been a devoted fan of that band for fifteen years and their music has provided me with more solace and comfort than almost any other music I listen to.

As much as I might not want to admit it, The Band Who Changed My Life was a goofy ska band from Denver, Colorado: Five Iron Frenzy.

(Pause for embarrassing silence.)

The Great Christian Ska Wars of the Mid-1990s[13] primarily involved two bands, the O. C. Supertones and Five Iron Frenzy, with a brief offensive launched by a band called the Insyderz, whose records include *Skalelluia* and *Skalelliua, Too!* The Supertones came out like they'd been thrown together by a Christian Malcolm McLaren. They had the look, the vibe, and the obnoxiously ska-y ska-titude of a ska band that is really into ska: the suits and skinny ties, the sunglasses, the name, the vocabulary ("rude boy" and "skankin'"), and most of all, the devotion to ska, which they constantly named-checked like a man declaring his love for a woman he's cheating on. I was really stoked the first time I heard the Supertones, the first time being, like most first times for me, in the early '90s, via a demo cassette at the Christian bookstore.[14]

The music wasn't bad, but I started to get suspicious by the time I got to the song "Found," on which the band lays out their three-point mission statement: "Preach the gospel, reach your heart, and ska ska ska ska." Another problem was that, at first, the Supertones' horn section lacked a trombone and trumpet, making do with just two badly honking saxophones. *Well, Supertones*, I thought, *I'm already familiar with the gospel, and I'm not really sure I want you to "reach my heart" if those saxophones are what you're going to reach it with.*

Contrast this to Five Iron Frenzy, a band who turned the safe, saccharine, family-friendly ethos of Christian radio on its head, who

13. Casualty estimates suggest that at least one hundred thousand record-buying American teenagers were affected by this tragedy, and untold hundreds more ended up with stupid hats.

14. Until my twenties, I thought that a band's "demo" meant the CD or cassette they let you listen to at the Christian bookstore for free, and not a short recording the band makes to try to get a record deal.

defied statistical improbability and found success in the Christian rock industry by blatantly championing Christian ideals[15] and writing prophetic (and hilarious) lyrics that challenged the worst of American Christendom, a band that curtly dismissed the ska genre on their first record, *Upbeats and Beatdowns*, with the song "Cool Enough for You." The thing about Five Iron Frenzy was that they weren't all about ska; they weren't all about preaching the gospel and reaching your heart, *per se*. They were just a good-ass band who loved Jesus and sang about some of the stuff he put them up to.

The first song on *Upbeats and Beatdowns* is about pioneers killing Native Americans. When I started reading the lyrics, I was like, *whoa*. By the time I got to the fourth track, "Anthem," which is about re-jecting American patriotism and pledging allegiance only to God, my mind was blown. I don't know how they did it—they mixed these thoughtfully subversive songs with songs about farts, dinosaurs, and video games. They even did an entire record of novelty songs called *Cheeses of Nazareth*. And above all, their music glowed with sin-cere, honest, heart-torn-out-of-your-chest-and-sewn-on-your-sleeve adoration of God. Fifteen years have passed since I first heard Five Iron Frenzy, and although I do not put on their records very often any more, "Kingdom of the Dinosaurs" still makes me laugh, "The Day We Killed" gives me chills, and it's impossible for me to make it through the final verses of "Every New Day" without weeping.

This is a band that made their career playing to evangelical Christian teenagers, selling records at Bible bookstores, and rocking shows in churches, yet they wrote songs that were anti-racist, anti-homophobic, anti-consumer, anti-Christian-music, anti-Christian-culture, anti-fame, and anti-corporate globalization. The secular metanarrative about CCM and Christian culture tells us that this should be surprising: Christians wouldn't like that; they wouldn't listen to it. But that's the big secret about why I loved Christian rock: we *do* like that, and we want to listen to it. Each Five Iron Frenzy song (except the ones about farts) was like a prophetic punch to the face. Evangelicals are supposed to be stodgy, closed-minded, and set in our

15. I don't mean Christian like "God wants everyone to have a nice family and not to watch R-rated movies"; I mean stuff like "Jesus is the Son of God who came to establish a revolutionary kingdom and died to save humanity."

ways, but—and I think the popularity of Five Iron Frenzy proves this— evangelicals are sometimes actually among the people most willing to change, most open to criticism, with ears most ready to hear that we are full of it and must change. We are open to a divine message that we need to shape up, and Five Iron Frenzy was there to provide it.

Five Iron Frenzy took me from a place where being a Christian was someone who I was, to a place where I had to face the fact that Christianity needed to be something I did if it were going to matter at all. Reese Roper's earnest screaming, whether about his own sin and loneliness or about the travesty of a world in which money matters more than people do, over the relentlessly chugging guitars and triumphant horn section: something about this music is a fire. If I hadn't heard Five Iron Frenzy, I don't think I would have been able to understand how music—even pop music, even ska (though they outgrew that genre rather quickly)—can so beautifully represent anguish and worship and justice.

Because Jesusy rock & roll is not the sheltered fantasy world some people think it is and some want it to be, if you're not careful, a Christian ska band may completely kick you in the brain and turn you into something you weren't before. It happened to me.

FIVE ALBUMS THAT SHAPED MY MUSICAL IDENTITY

 The Disciples, *No Options Here* (self-released)

The closest thing Christian music ever had to Mr. Bungle, a relentlessly spazzy, hyperactive, experimental band from a town where I used to live in California, was the cassette *No Options Here* by the California band the Disciples. This is some of the weirdest, best, goofiest shit ever made under the Christian rock umbrella. *No Options Here* is as brilliant as it is obnoxious and jokey. It's a Christian rock record that does not take itself seriously—it ends with the track "Twenty-Seven Seconds of Weirdness"—but maintains a straight face about the importance of ultimate questions. "Roaches" starts out as spoken word/jazz but disintegrates into roaring punk. "No Surfing in Hell" is obviously on message, but it is actually a *fun* song about the horror of being sent to never-ending torment. The best track is "Hard Tough Choice," because it's a straighforward song with a conservative Christian message (don't date non-Christians), but it bleeds emotion and sounds like a cross between the bands Faith No More and Bad Brains. Jason Sacks matter-of-factly sings, "You can't be my girl no more," but the music whirls, meanders, and turns in on itself, channeling confusion and uncertainty.

Poor Old Lu, *Sin* (Alarma, 1995)

Sin is unquestionably the epitome of the Christian grunge era.[16] And Christian rock, or any rock, has rarely seen a vocalist or lyricist like Scott Hunter. All his vocal sounds seem polyphonic, like he's always singing right at the break in his voice, between a low growl and a high falsetto, and what comes out is painfully pretty, a kind of delicate wheeze combined with an honest gravelly tenor. Hunter's lyrics, too, are opaque and abstract, capturing moods more than ideas, often ungrammatical and awkward. *Sin* is an exploration and explanation of a culture of suburban middle-class kids who are confused about how things work, about why we are so fucked up when we don't want to be, about why we never seem to be able to do what is right even when we think we know what is right. The record's most blistering track, "Bliss Is," is a short funk-punk tune about growing up in a family that doesn't communicate and how tension and anger bubbles beneath the surface. Aaron Sprinkle does so much with one guitar, his younger brother Jesse sounds like he's playing a one-thousand-piece drum set and yet every weird fill he plays feels absolutely necessary, Hunter sings about feeling suicidal and trapped by his family *even though he is a youth pastor*, and Nick Barber's nonchalant funk bass lines snake all over the place without even seeming to. John Goodmanson's production is dirty, angry, and vital. Why have you never heard this band?

---

16. To call *Sin* grunge is, I suppose, unfair, as *grunge* is a term that doesn't really mean anything other than a caricature of certain aesthetics typical of Seattle from the late '80s to the early '90s. And the band that most typified those characteristics for Christian rock might have actually been the New Zealand band Hoi Polloi, whose 1995 album *Happy Ever After* is basically a Hole album, but with better vocals and songwriting and production—it's just superior in every way. This is one of the few times that Christian rock borrowed tropes from mainstream music and actually made it better, not worse, in a timely fashion.

Five Iron Frenzy, *Our Newest Album Ever!* (5 Minute Walk, 1997)

Despite having shifted from a clearly pigeonholeable wacky genre band to a seething rock-with-horns juggernaut during their eight-year career, it was actually during the period when they were aggressively plying the guitar upticks of third-wave ska that Five Iron Frenzy made their best record. Like Reel Big Fish, a "secular" ska one-hit wonder in 1997, Five Iron Frenzy's second album (also released in 1997) had songs about selling out ("Handbook for the Sellout"), mocking themselves and people who would be so foolish as to admire them for being a ska band ("Superpowers"), and general self-deprecation ("Suckerpunch"). But while Reel Big Fish had only beer to numb the pain of self-loathing, Five Iron Frenzy combines a righteous rage against materialism, violence, and hypocrisy—themes touched on throughout the record and their entire catalog—with a longing and hunger for God. "Every New Day," the album's final song, was the band's perennial concert closer and an astounding thing for a late '90s ska band to be remembered for: a prayer and a reminder of God's unconditional love for all.

Genesis, *Invisible Touch* (Atlantic, 1986)

It's not as wimpy as *We Can't Dance*, but *Invisible Touch* is certainly Genesis at its most commercial, superficial, and pop-pandering. It's also a masterpiece, as any true pop fan—or, say, a fictional serial killer, like the protagonist of Bret Easton Ellis's *American Psycho*, who praises it as the band's best—can tell you. Rational arguments aside (Peter Gabriel was a more interesting singer than Phil Collins; prog rock is smarter than pop; "In Too Deep" is one of the cheesiest ballads of the '80s), *Invisible Touch* is the perfect mix of Phil Collins's hooky songwriting and the band's longstanding penchant for scary, labyrinthine compositions. See, for example, the two-part "Domino," which morphs from mournful love ballad to blood-soaked nightmare to pop anthem, or even "Land of Confusion," which manages to be dark, hopeful, and catchy all at once. For all its lightness—the twinkly guitars, Collins's meek vocals—there's a haunted spirituality hovering over the album, some kind of, well, invisible touch.

Michael W. Smith, *Go West Young Man* (Word, 1990)

Michael W. Smith is still making albums, having by now retreated back into the Christian culture cocoon from whence he came, but *Go West Young Man* is among his best records,[17] and it is also his first foray into the "secular" world, at a time when Christian pop stars were taking timid steps toward mainstream pop radio. "Place in This World" was Smith's Richard Marx-ish single—although "Richard Marx-ish" is an adjective that could be applied to at least ten years of Smith's career—and it caused a mini-Christian-controversy in the same way U2's "I Still Haven't Found What I'm Looking For" did: if he *really* knows the Lord so well, why can't he find his "place in this world," *hmmm*? "Place in This World" remains a refreshing glimpse of honest longing in mainstream Christian pop. A few other touches help elevate this record to something more than a grab for wordly radio play, like the soaring, hymn-like "Agnus Dei" (which is still sung in some evangelical churches) and the oddly soul-searching album closer "1990," a short, proggy meditation on Mark 8:36 (the bit about gaining the world and losing your soul). This final track offered a tantalizing glimpse of Smith's potential sell-out to secular temptations—which, of course, never manifested.

17. I never imagined I would say anything like this in my life.

3

High School Musical

THE DOUBLE LIFE

Consider the wearing of a Christian rock T-shirt to the average high school—the kind of thing I did when I'd gone to a Jars of Clay show the night before. On the one hand, I was pumped that I'd gotten to see these incredible bands that I so looked up to. But wait! Years of Sunday school and youth group training warned me: *Watch out, you are a minority. You are weird for being a Christian. People will make fun of you.* Wearing a Christian T-shirt to school resulted in the modern American equivalent of "being persecuted for your faith," which Jesus talks about in the Bible. I have a feeling that Jesus was more likely referring to martyrdom, but in the evangelical milieu of the 1990s this passage was also applied to people laughing at you for wearing a shirt that read, in the style of the Mountain Dew logo, "Jesus Meant to Die for You."[1]

Because of this, I kind of felt like I belonged to a secret club. When one of my junior high classmates found out we had the same favorite band, he did a double take, looked around, and asked, furtively, "Christian?"

"Uh, yeah," I replied.

---

1. If you can't keep up, please note that "Meant to Die for You" kind of sounds like "Mountain Dew."

He lit up. "High five!" I grudgingly obliged. "Do you like Rhythm and News?" he asked excitedly. I didn't have the heart to tell him that I didn't, and that "Rhythm and News" was the worst band name I had ever heard.

I was terrified about what might happen if I wore a Christian band T-shirt to school, though, and I even went to a *Christian*[2] high school. I'd get really embarrassed, totally red-faced, when someone asked me who Jars of Clay was. Matters were only made worse when one of the more uncool kids in newspaper class had actually heard of the band.

"Oh, yeah," he said. "Are they, like, Catholic rock?"

This was particularly mortifying. I knew Christian rock was uncool, but at least it wasn't *Catholic*. That would be even more uncool, more establishment.

CCM was built and is sustained by people who tend to understand "Christian" and "Catholic" as denoting two different religions. CCMers, evangelical Christians, don't call themselves "evangelicals"; we call ourselves "Christians," as if we represent the default normal way of doing Christianity—Jesus plus nothing—and others, like Catholics, add on a bunch of extra stuff that is weird and possibly wrong. I wasn't even aware that others might see this differently until I enrolled in a Catholic high school and the subject of religion came up with Gabe, a friend I made on my first day there. He and all of his friends had gone to Catholic schools their entire lives, but I was not Catholic and was therefore a novelty.

"So, what are you?" he asked.

I didn't understand the question.

"I mean, like, I'm Catholic. You're not Catholic, so what are you?"

"Nothing," I said. "Just Christian. Just regular."

That's how I felt as an evangelical at a Catholic school. Sometimes it was like I was weird for not being religious—I didn't go to the Friday masses, never crossed myself, didn't know when to sit or stand or kneel. And sometimes it was like I was weird for being religious—I listened to Christian music, went to church (not Mass) more than once a week, had a relationship with Jesus.

---

2. Technically a Catholic one, but Catholics are totally one thousand-million percent Christians, and if I exaggerate here it is only to make up for the nonsense some people give you to the contrary.

In a sense, I guess I lived a double life. You hear a lot from Christian teenagers about "living a double life." A double life is a really useful thing to have had, because it's something you can confess and come clean about when you "turn things around" and start to "get back on track with the Lord." The classic double life–repentance narrative involves a young man who goes to church on Sunday and youth group on Thursday, where he listens to worship music, prays, reads the Bible, loves God, and does wholesome things like seeing how many marshmallows he can fit inside his mouth or drinking other people's toothpaste water.[3] Then the rest of the week, he hangs out with his "secular" friends at his godless public school, swears, smokes, drinks, takes drugs, has sex, listens to Metallica, uses the Lord's name in vain, talks back to his parents, and tortures small animals for fun. Then he confesses all this at church camp in the summer, or maybe every Sunday, and eventually the cycle restarts.

In this sense, I have never lived a double life. I've always felt kind of jealous of people who did, though. Living a double life is such an important and understood signifier for some Christians that you don't even have to describe what it was you did. I was once in a Bible study with a guy who started to confess his past sins without being at all specific:

"I hung out with a bad crowd," he mumbled, his voice starting to quaver a bit. "I just started going down the wrong path."

He paused. Tears were coming into his eyes. People were nodding silently, supportively. "I've never told anyone this before," he said.

I thought this was the signal that his testimony was about to begin, but it was actually the end. That was it. He needed to get off his chest that he had hung out with some bad people and gone down the wrong path. Yet there was little confusion about what this path had entailed, because we all knew the story. I'm sure it involved secular music.

I, however, was pretty much the same person in high school as I was in youth group: a nerdy, shy, awkward smart-ass who was embarrassed by almost everything.[4] The only remotely duplicitous thing

---

3. This is a frequently performed Christian skit, the purpose of which I still do not understand.

4. I wish I could say things have changed in the last ten years.

I did was listen to alternative Christian music without telling any of my friends about it, because there was no one else in the world I knew who I thought would care. When most of my peers were listening to Nirvana on the one hand or Audio Adrenaline on the other, I was listening to Sixpence None the Richer. I only knew one other person who seemed to have similar musical tastes, and that was a college student who volunteered at my church named Charlie.

In the car on our way to some youth group event, probably yet another round of super-sugary desserts at a place like Red Robin, Charlie started telling us about his favorite bands. Charlie probably wasn't much older than we were, but he was a lot cooler, with his backward Kangol hat; slick, black page-boy hair; and pierced ears. He was talking excitedly about bands we'd all heard on the radio, in a tone of voice I now recognize in myself all the time. He gushed about the latest Primus single, the new Tool, the amazing double album that the Smashing Pumpkins had just released. And then, suddenly, as if an invisible voice had reminded him of something, this explosion of enthusiasm stopped midsentence.

"Of course, you guys know I would never buy any of these bands' albums," Charlie said. "I don't want to support that." We nodded approvingly. "What I'd really love is if one of those big bands like the Smashing Pumpkins[5] got saved and started telling people about the Lord."

The conversation quickly shifted to Christian alternative bands like Starflyer 59 and the Prayer Chain, and to be fair, they were great bands too. But clearly, Charlie had crossed a line, letting his secular sensibilities run away with him. His was a musical double life and he was in danger of leading us toward the wrong crowd and down the wrong path. Luckily, we had already arrived at the restaurant. Someone turned off the Newsboys album that had been playing, and we got out of the car, ready for a night of talking about Christian bands and eating ice cream.

5. Billy Corgan did have a kind of bizzaro conversion in the early part of the 2000s. Remember the Zwan album?

I DON'T WANT IT

Mine may have been the first generation of evangelical Christians raised on the idea that pop music was *not* bad to listen to or wrong; we were raised to think that it was only the *spirit* of secular music that was wrong. That is how we ended up with Christian versions of every possible obscure genre of pop music, even Christian splatter-core, which is a particularly bizarre subgenre of hardcore music characterized by whiplash-speed drums and guitars, a vocal style that is unironically referred to as "Cookie Monster," and lyrics that are principally concerned with gory dismemberment and brutal killing. The only Christian splattercore band I know of is Vomitorial Corpulence, who were from Australia, who sang about killing demons with an ax, and who can't have had more than four or five fans, because *really*.

The message was similar when it came to sex. It was not bad, not something to avoid or fear. Sex, we were taught, was good; it was great, in fact, after you were married. My pastor referred to himself as a "sex maniac" during a sermon about marriage, and I think it was only partly meant as a joke. But before you were married, it was something to be avoided. I believed this, but the timeline of desire was hard to follow: the day before your wedding, to sleep with your girlfriend would be a heinous sin that would cause you unimaginable trauma and pain, but the next day, it would be a sexy magic carpet ride with your one true God-ordained mate. Frankly, it was confusing. Plus, I get the feeling that my generation fell between two more aggressively conservative periods of sexual morality—there was no strict '50s-style puritanism, nor were there any flashy, twenty-first-century abstinence conventions like Silver Ring Thing, where they cut up stuff with a chainsaw on stage to show what premarital sex does to your heart.

What we had was True Love Waits, which is a card you could sign, with the following pledge on it:

> Believing that true love waits, I make a commitment to God, myself, my family, those I date, and my future mate to be sexually pure until the day I enter marriage.

We were presented with these cards at youth group once, and I wasn't totally sure what to do with mine. Like most teenagers who have read *Catcher in the Rye*, I was big on really *meaning* things, on rebelling against a society of phonies who would sign a pledge like this just because everyone else was doing it. I was no rebel, but if somebody tried to make me do something, I figured that was a good enough reason not to do it. I knew that after dinner I was supposed to do the dishes, yet if my parents asked me to do the dishes, it suddenly became a chore, or I felt I'd let somebody down because I hadn't leapt at the chance to do what I was supposed to do. I didn't want to be coerced into doing the right thing; I wanted to mean it. When it came to an abstinence pledge, I suspected I didn't even know what it meant to mean it. What did it mean to be sexually pure? Could I even have a girlfriend? Could I kiss her? If hugging a female friend leads to an unplanned erection,[6] should I leave off hugging all together? I didn't have a girlfriend yet, but not all of these were hypothetical questions.

I brought the True Love Waits card home with me and put it in the drawer next to my bed where I kept the letters I'd gotten from girls I liked and the poetry I'd written, whose chief themes were "why everyone except me and a few people I know are total phonies" and "why I love some girls who don't know who I am."

To be honest, even in my early teens, I didn't know a lot about sex other than what I had learned in grade school,[7] which was essentially the same education Arnold Schwarzenegger gives the children in *Kindergarten Cop*,[8] only it goes on for about two weeks, plus what I had learned from the book my parents gave me when I turned twelve, *Preparing for Adolescence: Caution—Changes Ahead* by Dr. James Dobson. Please keep in mind that in my home, like in most Christian homes, Dobson was an avuncular educator, not Hitler Jr. like he has been made out to be in other circles. His only crime as far as I knew was teaching me about sex through bland, straight-faced sentences

6. I suppose they were *all* unplanned, really.

7. For the sake of balance I should add that while we learned quite a bit in our classes, we learned just as much from the nudie pictures classmates smuggled in to school, although even those were confusing, because (a) we really couldn't be sure what the people in the pictures were doing, and (b) we were confused about what exactly was considered titillating, so one week we'd carefully examine a page somebody had torn from a *Playboy*, and the next week we'd ogle a scientific diagram from *Newsweek* explaining the warning signs of breast cancer.

8. "Boys have a penis, girls have a vagina."

like "The man's sex organ (his penis) becomes very hard and straight" and his description of orgasm as "a tingly feeling." I note with some dismay that this book appears to be out of print. I had assumed that this was still how Christian teenagers were learning about sex.

Of course, Dobson's book gave the usual Christian commentary on sex—it's a great way for a husband and wife to show that they love each other, but it is only ok between two married people. This was also the message from Christian music. Exhibit A: dc Talk's "I Don't Want It," the punch line of which was the repeated refrain "I don't want your sex for now." The truth is, it was almost a sexy song, with a groove that rivaled anything by C+C Music Factory. The lyrical hook had been panned to the left and right speakers so that if you turned off the left speaker, Toby McKeehan could be heard to say "I . . . want . . . your sex for now."

"I Don't Want It" was not the only abstinence anthem; there were plenty of others, especially Rebecca St. James's "Wait for Me," which is almost the polar opposite of "I Don't Want It." In romantic reverie, St. James sings to a fantasy future husband, whereas dc Talk's message was a lot more dude-ish, more like, "Yeah, chicks are hot, but don't have sex, because God doesn't want you to and that girl is a skank!" Or, as my dad once put it, "Would you really want to put your penis where some other man's penis has been?" It was a pretty compelling argument. Even my favorite band, PFR, had an abstinence song ("By Myself"), though it was (bias alert) much subtler than any of the others because it didn't even mention sex, just the emotional consequences of pursuing empty, temporary relationships.

None of these Christian sex songs would provide an accurate soundtrack to my own teenage romantic experience[9]—I kept the True Love Waits card in my drawer until I left home, never quite sure whether to sign it, and I graduated with almost all of my virginity remaining. For that reason, my favorite abstinence song was by a band called My Brother's Mother, a group formed by the guitarist from the Prayer Chain. They made a one-off album as a church worship band, laden with super-heavy, ultra-emotional songs about love. "How Do I Say No" is the stand-out track, but instead of being triumphant and righteous, it's broken and sad, a love song about wanting to do the

9. I wouldn't want to give Tal Bachman's "She's So High" that honor, but it comes a lot closer.

right thing after it's too late. It doesn't end with an argument for purity; it ends with "I just want you to hold me." It is a song that aches, and even before I had a girlfriend, I could feel that ache. I found this much easier to relate to—the deep longing, the regret—than a Rebecca St. James song. "How Do I Say No" speaks to those of us for whom being Christian also means acknowledging a great sad mess of believing things and not quite being able to make them work out the way we want them to.

That bittersweet ballad represented the fallout from the way that Christian rock takes love and sex so seriously and the way we learned, as evangelical teenagers, that sex was, basically, one of the biggest, best, more important things a person could do. Love is already a big deal at that age, when the emotional heaviness of even an unrequited crush threatens to drown us. Add to that the injunction from youth leaders to "keep the marriage bed holy," which meant that we needed to bravely face down desire, leaving our pubescent romances unconsummated. The result was a deep ocean of longing, not so much sublimated as directed toward a remorseful past or glorious future. Abstinence, it seems, makes the heart grow fonder.

FACING THE DEMONS

When I am not writing self-indulgent essays about Christian music, I spend a lot of time reading and writing about people speaking different languages, unfamiliar tongues, and being multilingual. In my Christian life, the idea of speaking in tongues has always been a little spooky to me, even though I technically grew up in a Pentecostal church. Strictly speaking, it was a Foursquare Church, which I used to find off-puttingly faux-hip, but lately have embraced because it was founded by a crazy Canadian lady who faked her own kidnapping and was married three times. The most important thing about Aimee Semple McPherson, who can in part be blamed for my life and this book, was her fearless embrace of new media—music, flashy lights, big shows, radio—this was how she got people to come to her church. It was how she talked about faith. A hundred years later, this is where I find my faith: songs, fog machines, and the agony and ecstasy of performance.

The Foursquare Church is, in theory, down with speaking in tongues. I say "in theory" because not only have I never done it, but I have never seen or heard anyone do it and I cannot remember it being mentioned during the ten or so years I went to the church. Lifecenter was a "seeker-friendly" church, which meant that a lot of the preaching focused on practical stuff about how to live your life and be happy, and not stuff about how you should speak some crazy language if you had really received the baptism of the Holy Spirit.

One thing that did get bandied about a lot, though, was demons. Our youth pastor once shared an anecdote about a suspiciously evil restaurant he'd visited on a trip out of town. "They had these desserts like 'Chocolate Sin,' and like 'Demon Chocolate Cake,'" he warned us. "I could feel a darkness there."

Darkness was frequently felt. Speculative anecdotes about demonic presence were passed around. One of my youth group friends whispered something to me he'd heard in his friend's church about a girl having sex with a demon. It was riveting stuff.

We were highly attuned to the idea of demon possession at one time in particular, and that was the yearly church camp held about an hour outside of Spokane, where we got together with students from five other local churches. Church camp felt about a million miles away from real life, spiritually.

You may have seen the rampant fundamentalism of *Jesus Camp*, but realize that for every Jesus Camp—there are not as many as you might think—there are dozens of camps that actually do a world of good to kids who need something, who go because their parents force them and who come out with a sense of identity, purpose, and peace that some teenagers desperately need, and that these things are not passed on through angry preaching and boot camp indoctrination but through love and conversations and songs. This is how it happened at the church camp I attended.

One thing you couldn't avoid, though, was the catch-22 of the camp's super spiritual atmosphere. Camp was the place where people dedicated or rededicated (you were pretty much going to do one or the other before you left) their lives to Christ, but all this Christ-loving was bound to get the devil angry, so he'd send his emissaries to try and muck it all up. The more you filled up on Jesus, the more likely the demons would come calling. And what better place for them to show up than in music? After all, the myth that Lucifer was the minister of music in heaven before he became the devil still holds currency in some evangelical circles. The devil may no longer have all the good music, but he's got a Flying V guitar and he knows how to use it.

I went to Christian camp twice. The first time, I met an amazing girl who I immediately fell in love with and there was magic everywhere and I loved God and I made friends with a guy who said he was a Christian vampire. I lay on the grass looking at the stars and talked about the Beatles with my new friends, and I heard Weezer for the first time, and it was basically the greatest week of my life. The second time, I looked everywhere for that same girl and never found her, our cabin leader gave us a long lecture on the evil of masturbation, and when I lost to a kid at air hockey he said, "Boy, you suck at everything, don't you?" It took me about five years to recover.

Probably the only good part of camp the second year was when I met a kid who was into metal and had recently become a Christian. He was a great guitarist, and we jammed together on Smashing Pumpkins and Jars of Clay songs. Like almost everyone who meant something to my spiritual life when I was a teenager, he has since disappeared, and I am left to wonder if he were even a real person. He had this puffy blond hair that made him look a lot like Beavis from *Beavis and Butt-Head*, which is an ironic thing for me to say because I had the exact same haircut. I liked this kid more than almost anybody I had met at a church-related event ever, because there was no bullshit about him. There wasn't much bullshit about most of the musicians I knew from church camp or youth group—Lisa, who truly loved God with all her heart, and Colin, who taught me how to play the guitar and never faked spiritual energy when he was playing, even when he looked miserable. Musicians were people I felt I could trust.

This kid—I think his name was Ian—had none of the stink of Christian culture on him, none of the practice of somebody who knew the right answers. He played me a song he had just written, about how he felt after he started going to church. I can still remember the chorus because it felt much more beautiful and true than the worship songs we were singing every night at camp. The song's chorus, which I still remember, went "and all you people are just turning me away / but just this once you will listen to what I have to say." I still find this haunting. In contrast, the camp's worship leader led us repeatedly in the truly dreadful "Romans 16:19 Says," which consists of everybody yelling, "ROMANS! SIXTEEN! NINETEEN! SAYS!" I cannot, in fact, tell you what Romans 16:19 says, because I got sick of the shouting after hearing it three nights in a row and have blocked it from my memory.

Ian and his music seemed to get at something that I felt—the idea that you could be a Christian but not like worship music or be good at air hockey—so we hung out, and blitzed through "Bullet with Butterfly Wings" by the Smashing Pumpkins. For the talent show night, Ian and I, and a couple of other weird kids we met, put together a punk rock ditty, which we played after Ian's song. Our main motivation for writing an impromptu punk song was that we wanted to rock out, but we also believed—and I still believe—that blistering noise was to the glory of God. The screamed lyrics to the three-chord, one-minute song, in their entirety, were "We will worship the son of God!"

One of the kids in our group was into Christian hardcore music, and in rehearsal, we decided it would be cool and funny if he got up and did a kind of free-verse hardcore vocal thing, cookie-monster style. He was supposed to growl a few lines about Jesus and then I would hit my cymbals and we'd be done.

The night of the performance, things were going great, and we breezed through the punk rock song all the way to the hardcore vox. Transfixed by the sheer absurdity of the throat-shredding roars, I watched my new friend, completely forgetting my signal to end the song. He continued the cookie-monstering for maybe ten or fifteen seconds before it was all over, and instead of applause, we were met with total silence.

The youth leaders looked at us with concern. Kids in the front row whispered to each other. The vibe in the room was less that of a punk rock audience than a family who's just been given bad news about a relative with cancer. Some adults quickly ushered us offstage.

"You shouldn't have done that," one of them said. We were mystified.

A few minutes later, we discovered the twin culprits: (1) demons and (2) rock music. According to the camp's leaders, the Cookie Monster kid had, in fact, been "demon possessed" (and, I assume, exorcized) only the night before. So upon hearing the throaty growls emanating from this sixteen-year-old at the microphone, everyone assumed it was not hardcore freestyling, but demons speaking through him. Wherever you stand on the question of spiritual warfare—I happen to think that whatever it is, it doesn't manifest in such a comic book form—this was at least an unfortunate misunderstanding and at worst a musical prejudice of the most heinous kind. Based on the evidence, it seemed that not a small number of the people in charge of the camp held a belief that a certain kind of music is verifiably satanic.

Full of righteous anger, we got together and made a plan to confront the camp's worship leader.

"We didn't do anything wrong," said Ian.

"Yeah, man," agreed the Cookie Monster kid. "I mean, it's just a style of music. I mean, I listen to Christian stuff like 'The Drowning Machine,'" he added, referring to a song by the Christian metal band Tourniquet.

I had to agree. "Listen, guys," I said. "We are totally in the right. All we have to do is go tell them what the song was about and why we did it." We knew our defense of distortion and growling probably didn't stand a chance, that we'd be rebuked, however gently, again.

Whatever happened—and to be honest, it didn't make enough of an impression for me to remember, fifteen years later, the conclusion to this anecdote—I know what kind of an impression this incident made on me. It was not that I should watch out for demons, or that it was wrong to make music that sounds evil to some people. It was that we have to believe that God understands our intentions, even when other well-meaning Christians do not. Ian, the Cookie Monster kid, and I spoke to God with tongues that were strange and unfamiliar to the leaders and the other campers. But the tongues we used to form those syllables of faith were our own. Given the myriad options available within the heteroglossolalia of the Protestant Christian lexicon, we'd found our voices in the growls and screams of rock & roll.

FIVE ALBUMS I OVERPLAYED IN HIGH SCHOOL

 Jars of Clay, *Much Afraid* (Essential/Silvertone, 1995)

A lot can be said about Jars of Clay, whose first album became an instant Christian rock classic. *Jars of Clay* is certainly not a bad album, though it's mostly a rehash of the demo the band made at Greenville College, which is to my knowledge the only college in the whole universe that actually offers a major in "contemporary Christian music." I'm not sure if any of the members of Jars of Clay majored in CCM, but they did hit on some magic formula that made them instant stars, even though they were just wienery Toad the Wet Sprocket fans with long hair and hemp necklaces and no drummer. *Much Afraid,* their second record, is actually their best. It has all the marks of the sophomore slump—the attempt to hang on to their previous fan base ("Frail" and "Weighed Down," recycled songs from their past efforts), the Judas-like "going electric" of the single "Crazy Times," featuring a wicked guitar solo with those note bends of two different notes that are almost the same, but not quite, and so sound totally awesome. The songs are simply great, and the record is much more concise and fleshed out than their debut. It's clearly an album made on the band's own terms, after their flash-in-the-pan MTV/radio success but before they were fully embraced by the CCM world. *Much Afraid* is both a tentative step into the world and a confident proclamation of faith.

The Smashing Pumpkins, *Mellon Collie and the Infinite Sadness* (1995, Virgin)

The '90s were a good decade for rock radio. Singles were churned out at breakneck speed, which makes it possible for me to call *Mellon Collie* one of my favorite records of the '90s even though, technically, I did not own it until I acquired it by marriage some ten years after its release. The soaring hope of "Tonight, Tonight" and "1979" are such a fitting soundtrack to my teenage years that I imagine they were always quietly playing on a radio somewhere at every significant moment—first kisses, spiritual discoveries, college admission. And the thick wall of distortion on this and every other rock record circa 1992–97 may be why my ears ring all the time now. Of course, it's "Bullet with Butterfly Wings" that almost defines post-grunge teen angst for my generation, and if I say I do not deeply and embarrassingly love every minute of that song—Billy Corgan's shape-shifting vocals (ironic deadpan to effete coo to bitter shriek), Jimmy Chamberlian's thundering and patently unnecessary drum fills, James Iha's anti-solo guitar chaos, the final cathartic "CAAAAAAAAAAAAAAAAAAAAAAAAAAAAAAGE!" of the bridge—I am a big fat liar. That the angst is spiritual—Corgan compares himself to Job and Jesus—only makes me love it more.

dc Talk, *Jesus Freak* (ForeFront, 1995)

This is the most important Christian rock record of all time. When it was released anybody who had been paying attention to music immediately noticed a suspiciously outdated Nirvana influence— suddenly Toby McKeehan was wearing a ripped cardigan and had messy blonde hair and a penetrating, listless stare. Yet *Jesus Freak* manages to be the apex of all Christian-culture baptized-pop-pastiche artifacts ever *and* to be a really good album of ten songs (minus the two interludes and Kevin Max's hidden poetry track), six of which were number-one Christian radio singles. *Jesus Freak* is a remarkably savvy mash-up of hip-hop, R & B, grunge, and radio-friendly pop. None of the songs are bad, unlike their previous effort, *Free At Last*.[10] What makes the record truly fascinating is that it is mostly not about God: this is an album about being an evangelical Christian. And it's done well, with artistry and grace and innovation, which is saying something for a band who used to crib lines directly from Public Enemy.

Weezer, *Weezer* (aka Blue Album; DGC, 1994)

There was nary a junior high or high school cafeteria that, at lunchtime, wasn't alive with the sound of five hundred young people "oooh-oooh"-ing along to "Buddy Holly." My own summer camp experience as a high school freshman was soundtracked by Weezer's "Undone—The Sweater Song," even though I wouldn't have bought their album at the time (I wouldn't become fully obsessed with the band for a few more years). No one who was young in the early '90s was untouched by the relentless singles of the *Blue Album*. This record, to me, is synonymous with sincerity, shyness, and love of the blossoming, nervous, as yet untouched and still unrequited (and therefore perfect) variety. It's an undeniably male record, and maybe a trifle misogynist in the way it relegates girls to the sphere of the imagination, placing them on

10. *CCM Magazine*'s Top 100 Christian albums of all time puts Amy Grant's *Lead Me On* at number one; *Free at Last*, which is mostly dreck apart from "The Hardway," at number nine; and *Jesus Freak* at number fourteen. The correct order is *Jesus Freak* at number seven and *Free at Last* in a cutout bin at a used record store.

unattainable pedestals or as ghostly figures in prom night fanta-
sies, but I can't think of a more accurate distillation of how it feels
to be a teenage boy. Plus, the guitar solos on "Only in Dreams"
completely kick ass.

Various artists, *The Winter of Our Discontent* (Tooth & Nail, 1994)

Tooth & Nail Records has been the unquestioned king of Christian
indie rock labels for nearly twenty years. Every important Christian band of my adolescence had some relationship to this Seattle
label, whose offices I later visited as an adult, when I found that
they were located in a nondescript gray building in a bland office
park near an upper-class neighborhood. *The Winter of Our Discontent* is the first compilation the label ever released, and it includes
songs from the first albums by Starflyer 59, MxPx, Blenderhead,
Wish for Eden, Havalina, and a handful of others. This record was
Tooth & Nail's first tentative step to the complete domination of
the Christian indie ("Chrindie") market they now enjoy and the
beginning of my "I love everything Tooth & Nail Records does"
phase. (Ask any evangelical male who grew up in the '90s—we
all had one.) I'd put up posters of Tooth & Nail bands I'd never
even heard, so great was my trust in this label. I even wrote and
mailed them a fan letter—the *label*, not the bands. I soon decided
I didn't have to love every record they put out (possibly after
hearing Plankeye). It warms my heart to know that, sixteen years
later, Starflyer 59 and MxPx are recording for Tooth & Nail. Some
things don't change.

4

I'm Gonna Love You Anyhow

WE'RE A BAND (BUT NEVER MIND THAT)

Christian rock almost became my religion. It feels weird, and a little liberating, to admit that. Like any number of American kids who were born born-again, I have been a Christian since I was zero years old. I've asked Jesus into my heart innumerable times, just to make sure he was still around. I've willingly attended Sunday school and then youth group when I was old enough. I don't know if youth group is still as strange a place as it used to be, if they still make you stuff marshmallows into your mouth and teach you that the earth is six thousand years old, but I think this is where I got the justification for my worship at the altar of Christian music. Youth pastors try hard, real hard, to keep kids on the right track, Godwise. I don't begrudge them that. It's their job, and maybe even their calling, to try to guide teenagers (who can be almost unbearably obnoxious at times) toward what is hopefully a healthy spiritual path. But because teenagers are, as a rule, so bitten by "the world," so anxious to be cool and to find a way to love and be loved, youth pastors have to try very hard to present something as compelling as keggers and video games. They have to find Christian coolness.

Thanks to advances in Christian coolness research, by the time the 1990s rolled around Christian coolness scientists had emerged from their laboratories with Christian rock bands that were a relative approximation of the stuff you could hear on regular radio stations. They looked and sounded almost the same, but they were somehow *moral*, and they were singing about God and Jesus instead of sex and drugs. Or sometimes about not having sex or about how drugs are bad. My youth pastor, I assume, subscribed to magazines that featured articles with titles like "How to Get Kids to Listen to Christian Music with Positive Moral Values," because here is how they got you:[1] they played this music all the time. They lent you CDs. They talked about the bands all the time. They organized trips to concerts. They put a lot of resources into making sure you were really into Christian rock, figuring that the rest would take care of itself, that you'd soak in the holiness and learn to look *through* the Christian bands to the source of their awesomeness, the Lord Himself. This, in fact, is a favorite trope of Christian rock bands—take, for example, Audio Adrenaline's "I'm Not the King (I Just Sing)" or "Never Gonna Be as Big as Jesus."

I'm not sure the rest did take care of itself. I don't remember picking up the Bible of my own volition when I was a teenager, but an entire wall of my bedroom was plastered with five years' worth of magazine clippings of my favorite Christian band. And I don't think it was all that wrong, to be honest. I needed something to revere, and these bands got me thinking about all kinds of ideas that I needed to be thinking about, including stuff that still matters to me to this day—love, mercy, justice, death, life, hope, joy, Jesus—so I don't think it was a huge problem.

Though I was an evangelical, I don't think I was ever a Christian fundamentalist, but I was definitely a Christian rock fundamentalist. At first, there was no doubt in my mind that it was wrong to listen to secular rock & roll, even if I sneaked a few listens to it on the radio from time to time. You may have heard the stories of fundies whose faith comes crashing down at the first possible hint of doubt, like Craig Thompson, the graphic novelist of *Blankets*, whose faith is destroyed when his pastor tells him that parts of Ecclesiastes—God's holy, unchanging, and inerrant word—were added later by scribes to make it a little happier. A radio story by Dave Dickerson, on *This American Life*, details his loss of faith when he discovered that a psychic wasn't demon-possessed, just a shyster. There's a long list of

---

1. Meaning me.

thirty-something artsy, writery types who grew up fundamentalist and had the spiritual rug pulled out from under them the minute somebody asserted that maybe Adam and Eve weren't literally the first two real human beings; they inevitably became instant atheists.

I am not one of them. I got, and get, confused about what it means to claim to follow Jesus, but leaving it behind, not being a Christian, simply does not compute. It is who I am. I did not "lose my religion." But I can remember the exact moment I lost my faith in Christian music.

In the '90s, if I was at a Christian concert, it's a good guess that Audio Adrenaline was the opening band. I'm not sure why they remained a warm-up act for so many years, but I saw them open for dc Talk and the Newsboys about a hundred times each, tour after tour. Audio A (as they were known to fans) had the corner, for a while, on the "rebellious" (yet supermainstream) quadrant of the Christian rock market. Like the other big Christian bands of their era—DeGarmo and Key, Newsboys, dc Talk—they were signed to ForeFront Records, a vaguely rock-oriented, incredibly safe label ensconced in the belly of the Nashville CCM beast. ForeFront played up Audio Adrenaline's bad-boy image—a genius move was releasing a live AA album under the title *Live Bootleg*, the cover of which displayed a *Maximum Rocknroll*–style, black-and-white photo of a band member headbanging in a totally righteous[2] way. There was nothing bootleg whatsoever about this record, although it did contain a recording of the band's live-only favorite "If You're Happy and You Know It (Bang Your Head)," which always made me feel slyly subversive—*this song isn't about God*[3] *at all, we are just banging our heads because it's fun!* Audio Adrenaline didn't even have a drummer on their first two records, but they were marketed as if they were a grunge or metal band. If you had to compare them to a regular rock band (and yes, you *had* to), you probably would have called them a "Christian Spin Doctors." Their

2. In the *Wayne's World* sense.

3. I was constantly cataloging which songs on my Christian rock records were not about God, as if I wanted to prove to myself that this was regular old rock & roll, just as cool as anything else at the record store, and that if my friends ever listened to it (which inevitably they wouldn't, since I'd been led to believe that nobody in America but me was a Christian), they would see just how cool it was.

ubiquitous Christian radio hit, "Big House" (about heaven, not jail), had the same sloppy four-chord party vibe as the Spin Doctors' "Two Princes," right down to the goofy scatting.[4]

Audio Adrenaline concerts were heavy on jumping around and shouting, especially on their Christian party anthem[5] "We're a Band," the chorus of which is, "We're Band! We're a Band! We're a Band!" Audio Adrenaline were, without a doubt, a band. And so their betrayal, which I experienced at a dc Talk show in the auditorium of Shadle Park High School in Spokane, hurt worse than almost anything I can imagine a Christian band having done. In the middle of the show, after forty-five minutes or so of sweaty headbanging and singing about how They Were a Band, Audio Adrenaline called for a little time-out to talk to the audience about Jesus. This wasn't at all uncommon at Christian concerts—in fact, I happily tolerated it when my favorite band, PFR, did this at their shows, even though I would never go up for the altar call. But when a guy with floppy, bleached-blonde hair and a turquoise Fender jazz bass stepped up to the mic, my life changed. And not in the way the band intended.

"I just want to tell you something," he said. We got quiet and reverent. "This music that we play—it's a trick. A trap." He went on to explain that the only reason they played rock music was to get our attention and tell us about accepting Jesus Christ as our personal savior. Jesus loves you, he said, and wants to have a relationship with you. The music is secondary, not the point; it's a snare. It doesn't matter.

It doesn't *matter*.

I was stunned. *It doesn't matter. The stuff I care about most doesn't matter.*

I started to feel angry. How *dare* you make me care about this music so much, how dare you—everyone, Christian record labels and radio and bookstores and bands and youth groups—how dare you make me fall in love with rock & roll and then tell me it's a farce, tell me that the only reason it's marginally ok that I'm listening to it is

4. Here's a scientific side-by-side comparison. Spin Doctors: "de-bee-bee-dip / da dap dip / da da da deebee dobee dobee dobee dobee dabbuh dobee daddah." Audio Adrenaline: "debee deebee da dap dap dow / hoo." Roughly.

5. That's the best way I can describe it, although such a thing cannot possibly exist.

that behind it all is the Right Thing to Believe. I already believe! Can I just have the music? And *you*, Audio Adrenaline, you said—you *just* said, a few minutes ago, in a song, over and over and over, that you were a band. *A band!* I had tolerated so many lame cultural trappings for this music I loved, but I would not tolerate a band lying to me. This was the beginning of the end.

CCM TO CMJ

After the betrayal, putting up with embarrassing radio shows and bad music started to feel less worthwhile, so I made a radical shift in magazine-buying habits: I went from *CCM* to *CMJ*. That may not sound like a huge difference—just one letter, really—but in terms of identity, it was everything. I now feel like the world posited by *CMJ* (*College Music Journal*) is just as full of crude posturing as *CCM* (though they don't do it in the name of Jesus), but at the time it was a big step, a coming of age almost.

The most important magazine I ever bought was the April 1997 issue of *CMJ New Music Monthly*. It came with a CD of current singles, which was my first, honest-to-goodness secular indie rock album. Sure, I'd bought a few "regular" pop records before—Sarah McLachlan, Superdrag, Five for Fighting[6]—but this was like entering a new world. Some of the songs on the CD included "Where You Get Love" by Matthew Sweet, Blur's "Song 2" (like so many Americans, this was the first Blur song I heard, though I now own all their albums), and White Town's "Your Woman."[7] Buried on the CD between a Christian indie rock band called Driver 8 and a bizarre concept project called World/Inferno Friendship Society is a song called "Rose Parade" by a singer named Elliott Smith. This was the late '90s and Smith had already been making music for a while, but I didn't know anything of this, hadn't heard of labels like Kill Rock Stars or Sub Pop, wouldn't have recognized band names like Quasi or Heatmiser. I lived in a parallel universe: I bought Poor Old Lu (not Nirvana) records, read *7ball* (not *Spin*), and

6. Shut up.

7. Let us pause to acknowledge, despite its utter lack of staying power, the greatness of this song, its gender confusion, and its hook, which totally sounds like the music that plays when Darth Vader is on screen.

listened to a syndicated radio show called *Z-Jam* (not *Z-Rock*, which was just down the dial). In my world, rock & roll was part of a package that included church, Teen Study Bibles, youth group, prayer, and evangelism. All of that was going to change soon enough. I had just bought my first *CMJ*, and it was full of indie rock and swear words.

I only heard "Rose Parade" once or twice for the first few months after I'd bought the magazine. I didn't usually get that far (track 20 of 21) in one sitting, but I had heard it, and there was something that struck me about it, something different than the kind of music I was used to hearing. It was very quiet, not really rock music at all (but certainly not folk), and had kind of an AM-radio feel to it—a comfortable fuzziness, a low buzz. I listened to a lot of AM radio—sports and politics, mostly—to lull me to sleep, so it felt warm and safe. I didn't know much about buzzwords like *lo-fi* and *four track*, but I knew that this was smaller and quieter than the other bands I was listening to at the time—MxPx, Five Iron Frenzy. Two other things struck me: one, Elliott Smith was the kind of singer I could file in my brain under "Stuff I Should Know in Order to Seem 'Underground' and 'In the Know,'" and two, I actually liked him and would not have to pretend he was not Christian in order for point one to work.

I had been doing this for a long time with Christian rock music: pretending that the reason no one had heard of my favorite bands was that they were so very *underground*, not because they were playing shows at churches and only sold their records at places that also sold votive candles and Bibles. The magazines I read did this, too—there were few (if any) references in the stories and reviews that suggested this music was anything other than simply too cool and good for those who didn't know about it. It was like being in the eye of a hurricane. Nobody mentioned we were a subculture because we were *Christian*, not because we were *indie*. This indie-by-religion thing worked pretty well until you had to actually start explaining who the bands were; I once found myself on a local radio call-in show decrying the idea of "mainstream music" and attempting to prove I was indie-minded because I listened to popular Christian rock bands. I was at my most dangerously sanctimonious, looking down on "mainstream" music not only because it did not jive with my values but because I "didn't care" about being "cool" and didn't listen to "the crap they play on

the radio" and I put "a lot of stuff" in "quotation marks" to show
how "ironically above it all" I was.

The conversation, on a day the host was talking about the com-
mercialization of music or MTV or some other pressing pop culture
issue of the day, went like this:

Host: OK, caller, go ahead.
  Me: Hi, yeah, well, I just want to challenge anyone to give any
       justification for listening to or liking any mainstream music
       for any reason.
Host: What do you mean, "mainstream music"?
  Me: You know, like anything on MTV, anything that's on the ra-
       dio, all that crap.
Host: So what kind of music do *you* listen to?
  Me: (*silence*) Um, you know, real underground stuff. The point is—
Host: Name one band that you like.
  Me: Well, uh, a lot of bands, there are a lot of independent labels,
       like Tooth & Nail . . .
Host: Tell me the name of a band.
  Me: I, well, you probably wouldn't have heard of[8]—
Host: (*hangs up*)

It would take me a while to stop thinking this way. Up until
the point that I bought that issue of *CMJ*, I clung to Christian music,
clung to it as if my life and faith depended on it. I remember one very
heated conversation with my best friend, Daniel, who by age fifteen
owned no fewer than forty David Bowie albums. I was severely limit-
ing myself, he said, by only listening to a tiny segment of recorded
music released by Christian labels. I knew he had a point, but I tried
to use his own reasoning against him.

"You just listen to a tiny segment of music, too," I argued. "You
just listen to Bowie and stuff related to Bowie, like King Crimson
and Brian Eno and . . ." as the list continued, I had to face it: the
great web of connections, for him, would never end; for me, they
ended when they hit the invisible walls surrounding Nashville. The
problem wasn't that I was only focusing on a tiny corner of the
world of pop music, because everybody does that. The problem was

8. The worst part is that I still kind of talk like this.

that I had let somebody else *tell* me exactly which tiny corner of music I ought to care about, and that those people had baited the hook with beliefs that had been with me my whole life. It was the most insidious kind of marketing, one that capitalized on a captive audience who loved Jesus.

I did the best I could to build a little world within this world I'd accepted, but I hadn't bothered to really take a step outside until "Rose Parade." Elliott Smith was my ticket to a more authentic claim of misunderstood hipness. During my *CMJ* phase, I started buying a lot of "non-Christian"[9] records, but Elliott Smith was the one who really expanded my world, who not only became a non-Christian staple of my CD collection, but who also enlarged my understanding of what and how and why I could love music regardless of religious and cultural lines drawn in the sand by record labels. Smith's music doesn't really have anything to do with Christianity *per se*, but he looms large in my history, he enlarged the reach of my spiritual and musical imagination, and to understand why you have to understand that Elliott Smith was the soundtrack to a Protestant boy falling in love with a Catholic girl.

XO

I only dated Catholic girls in high school. Not because I was *into* them as a type—our school was not of the repressed-sexuality-and-short-plaid-skirts variety[10]—but because they are the only game in town when you go to a Jesuit high school. My first girlfriend was a Catholic chick who drove a 1965 Ford Mustang, played the bass guitar, and listened to Depeche Mode. She was a total badass. It's unfortunate that I had no previous experience that involved being within ten feet of a girl and that the entire thing imploded, due entirely to my own cluelessness, after four months, one kiss, a mediocre rock band (me on drums, her on bass, Daniel on guitar, and nobody on vocals

9. We call pretty much everything that, FYI.

10. Not that this would have turned me on when I was in high school any-way. The Ideal Girlfriend template for evangelical teenage boys at the time was Rebecca St. James, a hot Australian singer who once made an album simply called *God* and who has written a number of books and songs about not having sex.

because we were too shy and nervous to sing), and an exchange of ska mixtapes.[11]

Things went better with my second Catholic girlfriend. She had long red hair and smelled like shampoo and whenever I saw her in second period band, her smile was beatific, beaming straight to my heart in the back of the room from up front with the clarinets.

This second Catholic girl, Serena, invited me to see *Good Will Hunting* with her, I think without romantic intentions, probably because she knew me as a fellow band geek (to say nothing of my involvement in a dubious extracurricular activity called Odyssey of the Mind), and we both took AP classes and were good spellers—the kind of people who would want to see a movie about a boy-genius janitor. We went to see the movie at Spokane's $1 Fox Theater, and there were times when I thought I should hold her hand, and I think she wondered the same thing, but the whole point here, the Elliott Smith part, is this: at a few key moments in the film—usually when Matt Damon's character, Will Hunting, is riding a train in the half-light of evening, looking sad and pensive because no one understands him— there is a soft, sad song playing on the soundtrack, a singer with a fragile voice, gentle like George Harrison (and wasn't he the sensitive one?). At the end of the movie as the credits are rolling and Will is on his way to California "to see about a girl," the drums and guitar kick in, lifting it above Smith's sad-sack acoustic lament, that lovely fragility lingering. The lyrics are probably about alcoholism and depression (the song is called "Miss Misery"[12]), but in the scene, the sadness is softened into hope, into the possibility that love is going to drive misery away.

Now was the time to draw out the unplayed Elliott Smith card. Would she be impressed? Would this Catholic girl see through my Protestant CCM-as-secretly-good-music facade and demand more?

11. I was heartbroken when she dumped me, for nonmusical reasons, but also she told me that she'd never actually liked Five Iron Frenzy. That was even more disheartening, because I had gotten *really* into Reel Big Fish for her, and their record was all swear words and beer and sex, so it was not easy for me to do.

12. As you know, "Miss Misery" was nominated for a Grammy but lost to Celine Dion's "My Heart Will Go On" from *Titanic*. There is another story here, about another girl who I saw that movie with, but it does not belong here because "My Heart Will Go On" has about as much emotional staying power and resonance as the experience of eating a Slim Jim does.

Best boy, gaffer, key grip, the song credits, and a name I recognized and suddenly: "Yeah! Elliott Smith! I *thought* that was Elliott Smith. He's good." Serena at least pretended to be interested, and the movie had heightened everybody's sense of Meaningful Quirky Romantic Stuff by about 75 percent, so I told her about "Rose Parade."

He's this singer, I said, from Portland; they play him on college radio. *She may be impressed*, I told myself. *I know about indie songwriters. I know about Portland. I know about college. I am cool. She maybe thinks I am cool.*

She maybe did think I was cool, and we began building a relationship on Elliott Smith and *Good Will Hunting* and a prom date a few weeks later. I started thinking that maybe I wasn't her first Protestant boyfriend, because she knew our lingo: somebody had talked to her about Jesus being her "personal savior," and you could tell it was in a serious way that meant, *Hey baby, I am concerned about your soul.* She said she didn't want Jesus to be her personal savior, which in my world was sacrilege. Of course, this doesn't mean "I don't believe in God" so much as it means "I am Catholic, so I will make out with you in your parents' driveway after we go to TCBY, but I am not about to go to an evangelical youth rally with you." The summer flew by in a fever dream of teenage hormones. Every action was imbued with meaning, every minute spent apart, a tragedy. Serena gave me a U2 mixtape full of the band's most religious (and sexy) songs; I took her to see MxPx and even bought her a Joy Electric record.[13]

Serena soon moved three thousand miles away for college, which was gut-wrenching, but also, in a way, stimulating. The problems that might have manifested didn't, because all we could do was miss each other and talk about how much we missed each other and write letters about how much we missed each other. No disagreements about whether it was called *Mass* or *church*, or whether or not you went on Saturday night or Sunday morning. No further embarrassment about the liturgical way her parents sang and prayed after dinner or the quickie preprandial Protestant prayer at my house.[14] No weird feelings if I wanted to go to a Christian rock show in the basement

13. No one should ever do this. But "Monosynth" is still a pretty good song, despite (or because of) its awesomely melodramatic conclusion in which the protagonist dies alone and misunderstood, his hands clutching a KORG.

14. "Thank you, Lord / For this food / In Jesus's name / Amen."

of the Methodist church but she wanted to go to a Catholic Workers' rights protest on the same night. We agreed on God, but we stuck to missing each other and kept our Sabbaths, as it were, separately.

Serena, in college, started to learn more about music than I knew. I only read magazines about "college radio," but already she was a DJ at her college's radio station, stealing rare singles for me,[15] sending tapes of her show playing bands I'd never heard of—the Stooges? G. Love and Special Sauce? This stuff is *amazing!*[16] For my eighteenth birthday she sent me a copy of Elliott Smith's new album, *XO*. It seeped into my soul, the warm, organic, cedar feel of it, the serene doubled vocals, the ecstatic misery. I was an evangelical Protestant high school kid listening to secular music and in love with a Catholic college girl. My world was getting bigger.

We loved hard, like only eighteen-year-olds can, like nothing is more important than *feelings,* but I was on one side of the country in one Washington and she was on the other side in another Washington. When I finally got to visit Serena on spring break—my parents agreed to it if I brought along Daniel as an ersatz chaperone—things had unraveled.

She let us host her radio show, which was something of a lifetime goal. Daniel played some pop songs by Fuel and Fretblanket (he had oddly taken a shine to all of the middle-of-the-road pop rock bands discovered and then forgotten by radio, the ones you still see in used CD bins today); I played My Bloody Valentine and Starflyer 59. And for some reason there was one other song I really wanted to play, maybe because I was prescient of overhanging doom.

"I know that most of you out there are probably feeling pretty good right now," I said into the microphone, all my teenage radio dreams coming true while Serena did homework in the booth behind us. "But you need to know that not everybody feels as good as you do." I'm sure I was right. It was a sunny day; they were in college, rich, privileged, and going to parties that night. Vacation was coming up. But the song: "So Low" by Self. Self is a great band and a total one-hit wonder in terms of commercial radio, which is all the more

15. This is not as big a deal as it sounds. I mean, come on, you steal mp3s, right?

16. Look, "Baby's Got Sauce" is still a great song, so shut up.

wondrous in that their one hit is about a guy who is so depressed he's wishing for "a knife in my chest / and a bullet in my head."

It's a really *catchy* death wish.

I didn't feel this song at all. I had never in my life felt that low, but I was about to. My musical instincts knew what my brain and heart didn't: I nodded my head to the relentless beat, rocking out to the song, but Serena and I were separated by a glass wall—she couldn't hear the music—and moreover, I later learned, she was already long gone, had fallen hard for a Catholic senior she'd met at a party. MxPx and Sixpence cannot compete, even Elliott Smith cannot compete, with somebody who comes from the same place you do.

That night, we were in her dorm room, curled up on her bed, awkward and confused, full of love and bad vibrations, Daniel banished to the next dorm room, watching *Gone with the Wind*.[17]

"I don't think this is going to work," she said.

"Why not?" I said.

"I just don't think it's going to work."

There were a lot of other things she could have said. I think this was the safest choice, even though it threw me into a swamp of confusion that it took me the better part of a summer to recover from. I remember the rest of the DC trip like a badly smudged pencil drawing. Daniel and I wandered aimlessly through the city and went to some museums, about which I can recall nothing, and I bought the Dutch indie rock band Bettie Serveert's album *Palomine* at an independent record store, which I remember quite clearly.[18] An elderly, homeless man staggered past us and pointed at me. "The CIA has a file on you," he slurred. I don't know what would have been in it—probably just my report cards and maybe some parking tickets. I hadn't amassed that much official documentation yet—adulthood was a world away, and this new world of apartment keys and parties in DC was a world I was visiting and did not understand.[19] The only file I had was a manila envelope thick with

17. "Do you know how long *Gone with the Wind* is?" he later asked. "*Four hours.*"

18. Perhaps it says something about me that I can remember exactly what record I bought that day but couldn't figure out that my girlfriend was in love with someone else.

19. The first time I heard "The District Sleeps Alone Tonight" by the Postal Service, I was stunned, because its lyrics are a completely accurate account of what happened to me on this trip.

letters from Serena, sent from her work-study office with free postage, which I suspect is a federal crime, but this was teenage love!

Right: *Was. Had been.* Somehow, I knew, there had been something like love here. We cared about Elliott Smith and each other. The important difference is that I was a high school kid from Spokane and she was a college student on the East Coast. And she was falling in love with the man who would become her husband and the father of her children.

The week ended unceremoniously, except for the fact that I now had a giant Serena-shaped hole in my heart, along with the God-shaped one U2 sang about on their *Pop* record, which she'd given me as a gift. I went home and tried to forget about it, attempting to transfer my affections to an unattainable flutist in second-period band. I put on *XO* whenever I had to write a research paper—the AM radio buzz was still soothing, even though the pain in the songs was more acute.

I called Serena, years later, the day I heard Elliott Smith had died. She had heard about it, she said, but her grandfather had died on the same day—he had been sick for years—and she had more to grieve over than what *From a Basement on the Hill* would have sounded like in its intended form. I had never met Serena's grandfather, or Elliott Smith, and it felt somehow hollow that the latter mattered more to me. I hadn't even known who her grandfather was, or where he lived, or that he was sick. That love that had seemed so deep and wide and desperate, that seemed to bridge schisms of distance and religion, now suddenly seemed like a pale shadow compared to the mundane, lovely, and unshakable edifice my new wife and I were building.

After I hung up, all I could think of was the refrain of Smith's "Waltz #2": "I'm never gonna know you now, but I'm gonna love you anyhow." I wondered who exactly I was feeling that about.

Elliott Smith was gone, and when I'd seen him play a show a few years earlier, he seemed confused and distant. Confused and distant was how I'd felt, too, back when I was on the plane home from DC. Serena was miles away, spiritually, temporally, physically. I hadn't even gotten to know God that well, even as I pseudo-evangelized Serena with Christian punk rock records—he was hiding in songs, and hiding in a deeper and more complex way now that I was listening to non-Christian music. I was eighteen years old, and I didn't know anything —not well. But if I learned anything from Elliott Smith, it's that you don't have to try so hard at the knowing; you can skip straight to the love. And the love, my love for a sad guy with a guitar and a pretty girl in a long green skirt and the Source of all this goodness and beauty— that was all I needed.

FIVE ALBUMS THAT CROSS THE CHRISTIAN-SECULAR ABYSS

Audio Adrenaline, *Don't Censor Me* (Forefront, 1993)

Don't Censor Me is a tangled mess of genres and ideas, even for a Christian rock album. "We're a Band," a declaration of AA's intention to use rock music for God, really doesn't sound like rock at all, but like a hip-hop party anthem. "Jesus and the California Kid" is an absolute *mess*: the verses are freaked-out raps over elastic guitars, straight from the Red Hot Chili Peppers hymnal, while the chorus is a Beach Boys homage. The song reminds us that although Jesus was not a surfer dude who drove a Corvette, he died for the "California Kid," a character who remains nearly anonymous, but who couldn't *possibly* be Christian, what with all that surfing and whatnot, and who—surprise!—isn't beyond redemption after all. The title track suggests that it's Christian bands who are getting the bad rap for their lyrics, being censored by those do-badders who'd rather have our kids exposed to S-E-X than hear about this God that most people call "the Lord." The record had some genuinely good songs on it too, mostly the ballads. "My World View," which featured Kevin Max (the "rebellious" member of dc Talk) and which is not about creationism or anything, is a pretty ballad about seeing all of life and time at once. "Rest Easy" is almost a U2 song about being weary and resting in God, and it is pretty even though it takes the unfortunate path of having God be the speaker in the chorus. And even "Scum Sweetheart," which is a Christian song about being disappointed by "the world," slinks around with sexy blues riffs and becomes something genuinely, sinisterly cool.

Superdrag, *Regretfully Yours* (Elektra, 1996)

It is cliché to say that God has a sense of humor, but if you have ever tried to do anything, you might surmise that he is at least somewhat fond of irony. Take Superdrag, for instance. "Sucked Out" is hands down one of the best disposable power-pop singles of the '90s, and although it was tacked on to this noisy pop record, the whole album, from the LP-era aesthetics to the honest, scratchy vocals, was just plain classy. The moral dilemma here was with "What If You Don't Fly," the only remotely theological song in the bunch (the rest are mostly about girls and smoking cigarettes). The song timidly—quite timidly—suggests that maybe there isn't a heaven, or at least maybe that the addressee isn't going to go there: "Cause when you die, woah, what if you don't fly." How could I listen to this and be a believer? I got evil butterflies in my stomach whenever this song came on. Ten years later, John Davis, who wrote that song, had his Damascus moment, converted to hardcore evangelical Christianity, put out a few superreligious solo albums, and eventually, as a Christian, re-formed Superdrag. So, note to sixteen-year-old self: go ahead.

Starflyer 59, *Gold* (Tooth & Nail, 1995)

Jason Martin has been making rock albums under the name Starflyer 59 since 1994. Every album has been made under contract with Tooth & Nail Records (he and his brother Ronnie Martin's Joy Electric must be the label's longest running artists) and has almost never made any music that sounds like "Christian rock." The first Starflyer records, including the best, *Gold*, were mired in misery over women, buried under a wall of distortion the likes of which could make My Bloody Valentine's Kevin Shields reach for earplugs. This music is probably more dangerous for teenagers than something like Eminem—at least you know he can't be serious when he talks about wanting to rape and kill his own mother, but there's no warning on *Gold* against the seductive, life-sucking power of feeling sorry for yourself because the cutest girl in your high school is not in love with you. The deepest most awful feeling I ever felt when I was a teenager was listening to "One Shot Juanita" the night before my girlfriend moved across the country to go to college. I drove home choking on my own mucus, barely able to see the road. Starflyer gradually got over it[20]—Martin eventually got married[21] and had some kids and took over his father's trucking business. The liner notes for *Gold*, like every other Starflyer album since, include the words "ALL PRAISE AND GLORY TO JESUS CHRIST OUR LORD AND SAVIOR," but the album is pure sadness, reaching its zenith during the nearly seven minutes of "Messed Up over You," the interminable instrumental

20. So did I, obviously.

21. After a brief relationship with Sixpence None the Richer's Leigh Nash. This seems significant, somehow.

section of which is a funereal church organ playing a minor-key progression while Martin's guitar wails unadulterated self-pity, a kind of "While My Guitar Gut-Shakingly Sobs." It's beautiful.

MxPx, *Life in General* (Tooth & Nail, 1996)

You would think *Teenage Politics* would be MxPx's ultimate teenage anthem record, but no, it is *Life in General*, by leaps and bounds. The band hit their pop-punk stride here, thanks to Steve Kravac, and they then kept it up through a string of two more excellent, creative records (*Slowly Going the Way of the Buffalo* and *The Ever Passing Moment*) before they burned out. The members of MxPx are only about three years older than I am, which made them a convenient source of unrequited love and angst songs to fuel my longings. "Do Your Feet Hurt" is a punk rock song built on an old pickup line ("Do your feet hurt? Because you've been running through my mind all day"), and by the time it got to its 6/8 doo-wop-style breakdown (and coincidentally the record's only actual mention of God), they had me convinced that they'd hit on the purest pop expression of love possible. If I had to pick a record to represent a late high school summer, with all its sunshine and possibility and romance and angst, it would be this one. There is not a bad song on it.

Elliott Smith, *XO* (DreamWorks, 1998)

XO is Elliott Smith's major-label debut, which is supposed to garner cries of *sell-out*, but I just see it as a guy finally getting the resources he needed to make a great-sounding record. There are no songs from *Good Will Hunting* on *XO* (most of those were taken from *Roman Candle*), but there are a lot of love songs and sad ruminations on existence, like on "Amity," in which Smith contemplates the old saw "God don't make no junk" and wonders why it is, if that's true, that he himself exists. The record ends with the most starkly pretty statement of the pain of living I had ever heard in my eighteen years, a gorgeous multi-tracked falsetto chorus of Elliott Smith singing, "I always feel like shit." This record is light on its feet, with nimble acoustic guitars and gently plunked piano, but it's heavy, and it made me feel like a grown-up who had heaviness to deal with, like the fact that the person who bought me the record was a hot college girl and our relationship was getting complicated and weird. *XO* is one of very few records I had when I was eighteen that I still have now.

5

Everything All the Time

HOW THE INTERNET SAVED AND DESTROYED MUSIC
FOR MY GENERATION

If writing about music is like dancing about architecture,[1] then writing in a book about the Internet is like . . . uh, well, it's weird. And it's really hard. Is there anything the Internet is not about? Is there anything that's not on the Internet? I live in a world in which things somehow gain legitimacy by being represented via a vast computer network, a network that transforms things that were perfectly fine for a million jillion years into fodder for online message boards. I am a product of my age: if something is not on the Internet, I assume it is not knowable. The computer is the first place I turn with questions factual and immaterial; I have googled everything from "My Bloody Valentine lyrics" to "How to tell if a woman is pregnant." (Let me tell you, understanding one is just as hard as the other.) And if there is one thing I use the Internet for more than any other, it is music.

The World Wide Web has fundamentally changed the way I interact with and understand pop music. It has made music better and more accessible in many ways, but it has also made the experience of listening to and buying and liking music feel tiring and pointless. Almost everyone who loves music is completely oriented toward the

1. Which it isn't.

Internet now: it is the origin of official press releases and of all grass-roots, word-of-mouth buzz. It is where we acquire our music. And so it is where we are instead of at the record store. It's cool to be able to easily tap into all that information and to find those recordings—like, for example, right now I am listening to a 1971 record made by a Unitarian church that I never could have possibly heard without the Internet—but it's not very cool to sit and stare at a backlit box when you're looking to find out something about a vital art you love and that moves you. There is so little movement when one is sitting on one's ass, mouth agape, in front of a computer.

You may not believe me, but there was, boys and girls, a time before the Internet. You kids today with your iPods and your Web 2.0 and your Wi-Fi connections may not realize that those things have not always existed. The Internet is a thing that somebody invented, and, at first, it was really expensive.[2] My family did not have access to the Internet at home. We had a tiny black-and-white Macintosh computer, which I used for playing a game called "Dungeon of Doom." I had *heard* of the Internet, and I knew of some places where you could "log on" to this newfangled "information superhighway." Our computer even had a program on it that, as far as I could tell, would somehow connect the computer to something bigger if you clicked on it. The program never actually connected to anything—you needed extra hardware for that—but psychically, people of my generation were ready for what would be coming soon enough: a magic button that allowed all the information in the world to fly through the air and appear on a screen in front of you. And so I sat before the computer, opened the program, and watched as it displayed a little box of text that read "Connecting . . . ," willing it to somehow connect to "the Net,"[3] where I would, I hoped, get a lot of information about music, which was my main interest apart from girls and Dungeon of Doom.

Today, humans mostly use the Internet casually, for research, pornography, and something called "tweeting," but when the world was young, in 1994, we used it desperately, taking what precious little time we had to go on "information runs" the way you go to

2. The same goes for CD duplicators, which used to cost like $600. Although you might not even know what CDs are. I wish I were joking about this, but I recently saw a Sony Discman in a museum, so I cannot be sure.

3. Starring Sandra Bullock.

the grocery store for dinner ingredients when there's no food in the house. There was nowhere else to get the information we wanted—discographies, song lyrics, guitar tabs, bands' addresses.[4]

My friend Daniel and I started checking out the Internet at our local library, where you had to take a class on how to use the Netscape browser before you were allowed to use it. Even though anyone under the age of thirty instantly knew exactly what to do within five seconds of looking at the browser, the librarian carefully explained the function of such buttons as *Stop*, *Back*, *Forward*, and *Refresh* while adults nodded their heads thoughtfully. We passed the class and got special endorsements on our library cards that allowed us to sign up for times to use the Internet-enabled computers. The sign-ups had to be done—brace yourself—by phone or with a pencil and paper at the actual library.

We did finally get online, and I started to learn more about what was out there in the world of music—Christian music, at least, which was my world. My favorite Web sites circa 1994–96 were Christian music sites, and in particular a "chat" (in a very loose and primitive sense that involved clicking the *Refresh* button a lot) site called NetCentral. NetCentral was a Christian music Web site that was fairly indiscriminate in the things it promoted: these were the days when CCM felt small enough for us all to sense (as we still sometimes do) that we were all on the same team, and so they promoted everything from adult contemporary to hardcore punk. I logged in to NetCentral almost every time I went to the library, and under the name "poor-oldlu," I discussed Christian rock with other nerds who were just learning how to use the Internet. Daniel, who was a bit more savvy than I (and tolerated or even liked some of my favorite Christian rock bands), showed me how it was done.

We'd recently discovered a Christian grunge band called Johnny Q. Public, who'd played a show for about five people in a Christian bookstore's parking lot in Spokane a month or so before, and we were eager to discuss them.

"Anybody heard of Johnny Q Public?" I typed. "They are kind of a hard rock band."

One kid typed back, "I hate hevvy metel crap!"

A jolt of nerdy enthusiasm shot through me—was I actually going to get to discuss music I thought was great, music that no one else

4. Actual, physical addresses!

I knew knew about. Somebody disagreed with me, and if I wanted to, I could eviscerate him.

"Their awesome!" someone else typed.

There were other people in the world who had heard of Johnny Q. Public and I was talking to them! The world was born anew until Daniel set me straight. "OK, now what we do is we pretend we *are* Johnny Q. Public," he explained. "That's what the Internet is for. It'll be fun. We'll talk about how, like, we're on tour and stuff."

This didn't seem right to me—that would be lying! But he was right: about the first ten years of the Internet seemed to be devoted to trying to figure out if the guy pretending to be Rivers Cuomo[5] really was Rivers Cuomo (he wasn't). Online music culture has become more honest and transparent since it first began, and now Rivers Cuomo has MySpace and YouTube accounts, and he really is him—celebrities are pretty much required to have their own verified Twitter account.

I remember very little about those chats, except that it was exciting to connect with a community of people who cared about the same obscure music I did, which probably forever colored my idea that the Internet is a good place to do that kind of thing.[6] The other thing I remember is a sentence I typed to someone who asked for my e-mail address (and who I now assume was a sexual predator) after a discussion we'd had about music. I really seemed to know my stuff, he/she said, did I want to talk more? I said I didn't, or couldn't, as I didn't have an e-mail address. But "I really wanna work in the CCM industry when I'm older."

I can see those words appearing on the screen: I said that, I wrote that. I was or am a person for whom working for a Christian record company or magazine or band was a goal, a dream, even. I remember getting the catalog for Tooth & Nail Records by mail order, looking at the hip photos of the staff, and thinking: I would love to be those people. Music is their job. And not just any music: Christian rock, music that glorifies the Lord. How awesome would it be to have a job that involved rock & roll music made for God? Was there anything else worthwhile in this world? I loved the idea that I lived in a world where it was possible, in theory, to make a living as part of that team.

5. Frontman of formerly awesome band Weezer.

6. I still do it every once in a while at a Web site called ArtsandFaith.com.

The *team*. I keep coming back to that word, because that is what being an evangelical Christian in 1995 felt like: we were all on a team together, all fifty million or however many of us there were, and we helped each other. We built things like bookstores, schools, magazines, bands, and churches. We could be nice to people who were not on the team, be friends (though not "unequally yoked"), but ultimately, we were in this together and they weren't, so we huddled together, not because we were persecuted (although we may have claimed the contrary), but because we really did gain strength and courage and comfort from one another; we really believed in the same thing. And we believed that making music about who we were, which was Christians, was the right and good thing to do and that it would positively impact the world.

I don't think we were wrong. Now I find Christian culture foreign and ghettoish, and I don't like most Christian music. But the idea of Christian rock music, even, seems to have disappeared. The Internet still has its Christian communities, but the world in which Christian music is all you listen to, where you can say a band sounds like Phil Keaggy when they actually sound like the Beatles, seems to have disappeared, and the Internet has been in no small way responsible for removing those barriers between musical cultures. I'm mostly happy about this, but I also can't help feeling like a house I used to live in has been torn down. And the way music communities, Christian or not, exist online now feels alien and confusing. We are anonymous users scrambling to steal new releases, say mean things to each other about our favorite bands, and prove who has the biggest hard drive full of unreleased Weezer rarities.

This started, I think, the day we discovered Napster.[7]

MUSIC NOW

There are few historical events of my lifetime embedded firmly in my brain: I remember watching the news when the Berlin Wall was torn down. I remember Bill Clinton's inauguration. I remember that I was at the post office on September 11 and I heard something on the

7. For the benefit of younger readers, Napster was what we used to steal music before torrents were invented.

radio that I mistakenly believed was a report that the Port of Seattle was closed due to a bomb threat. I also remember, with crystal clarity, the day I first heard about Napster, which changed my life perhaps more than any of those other events did. I recently told this story to a group of college students, all of whom were born in 1990 and have never known a world where you couldn't immediately get a hold of any recorded music or film that you wanted, for free, instantly. The impact of this moment, needless to say, was lost on them.

How can I put this? Imagine starving for twenty years, maybe eating rice cakes and peanut butter, which you purchased after saving up a small amount of money every couple of months. Then imagine that, suddenly, you are given a magical refrigerator that is always full of whatever food you happen to be craving at that very moment and then gorging yourself at every opportunity. That is what it was like.

I was not the first person I knew to discover this magical refrigerator, so to speak. Daniel was a lot more connected to pop culture than I was, because (a) he had MTV and (b) he was Catholic, and so he had avoided the Christian culture ghetto—although he did have some cassette tapes of priests singing Hail Marys and something about the Fires of Hell. Daniel had his finger on the pulse of Hot New Stuff outside the tiny pop world I lived in, and I remember getting excited phone calls from him about new pop-culture phenomena as they occurred. He'd be up watching *120 Minutes* at two in the morning on a school night, and I'd get calls like: "I don't know how to describe this song—it's like acoustic, and there's a saxophone, and in the video there's this crazy woman dressed up like a clown, and it's awesome" (Dave Matthews Band). Or "Man, I just saw this new band; they're like, I don't know, they're like Silverchair, only younger, and worse" (Hanson). In 1997, he discovered Radiohead: "I just bought this CD, and the cover is so weird and cool. It's like this time-lapse photograph, this fast-motion kind of thing, and it kind of looks like a highway, and man, it's so awesome."

One day he called me, the summer we had just graduated from high school, to reveal a new piece of information that wasn't about a record or a band. It was, as we'd soon find out, about every record and every band, ever.

"Joel, check this out," he said. "I just found this new thing on the Internet. It's amazing. What you do is, you type in the name of a song, and then the song is on your computer."

I didn't say anything for a few seconds, trying to sort out the meaning of what I'd just heard. I knew we were talking about music, but something was not making sense. He had said that you could listen to a song, but on your computer. Songs, I knew, could be listened to on records, cassettes, and CDs, but the nearest I'd come to hearing music on a computer were the eight-bit theme songs to games like Oregon Trail.

The closest thing we had to music on the Internet before this was a service called 1-800-MUSIC-NOW, which only lasted for a year but which—are you ready for this?—was basically a music-buying Web site, except *on the phone*. You'd call up and punch in the first few letters of a band you liked, and then they'd play a sample of it for you, over the phone, and you could order the CD by pushing a few more buttons. Daniel and I called 1-800-MUSIC-NOW dozens of times a week, especially on Monday nights, waiting for them to release the sound clips of the following day's new releases, the latest PFR or dc Talk or Newsboys albums.

But this new thing Daniel was talking about sounded different, a lot different. Songs. On a computer. How can a *song* be *on a computer*?

"Daniel," I said. "A song cannot be 'on a computer.' A song is not—I mean, it's not like a thing that can be—what do you mean, the song is on your computer? Is it like a Web site?"

"No, it's not a Web site," he claimed. "You just search for a song, and then you click on it. You have to leave it connected to the Internet all night, but in, like, twelve hours, the song is downloaded to your computer and you can listen to it."

"Daniel," I pleaded. "This does *not* make any sense. At all. I don't even know what you're talking about. Your computer just finds something that isn't on a Web site?" Were there just songs floating around out there somewhere in the ether, like the music of the spheres? Was a modem something we had invented that could just pluck a song out of nowhere and allow us to possess it?

"Just come over and try it."

I did. This was not any kind of Internet I had experienced before: there was a box on the screen where I could type the name of a singer or band I liked, and then a list of songs (where were they?) would show up. I typed in "Jeff Buckley" and not only did I get a list of songs I knew by him, I also got a bunch of songs I had never heard of, like "Forget Her," which was cut from his first album. And I got weird live recordings from New York City when Buckley was playing with Gary Lucas's band, and I got Smiths covers. You just clicked on the song, and within about twelve hours (this was way pre-DSL) it was, in fact, on your computer. All over the country—the world—other kids were discovering this same miracle. And we all went completely bonkers.

The Napster revolution happened to coincide with college, for me, and college meant, among other things, insanely fast Internet for free. Because the people who ran things were at first pretty clueless about our insatiable desire to possess all music ever recorded, this meant that thousands of college students had unfettered freedom to download kazillions of megabytes of music data all the time. It was like being given a shopping spree at Tower Records, only without the shopping. The urgency was still there, though—not the urgency of only having five minutes to grab as many records as possible, but the urgency to *know*, which is probably what college is supposed to be for. Although I think I was supposed to be studying Aristotle and Milton rather than the Smiths and Wire. Somebody would mention a band, and *bam*, you instantly downloaded their entire catalog. It was exhaustive and exhausting.

We also started discovering amazing rare mp3s that were too good to be true, because they *weren't* true. I'd still like to slap whoever had the idea to label the artist of a song as "Weezer, Tom Petty, and the Counting Crows," three artists whom I'm sure have never even been in the same room together. There were millions of songs like that, floating around on the Internet, forever incorrect, probably more the product of desire than deceit. Who wouldn't want to think that all their favorite bands had gotten together to record? We'd download tracks like "LIVE RARE UNRELEASED Björk and the Rolling Stones featuring Metallica, Patti Smith, Frank Black, and My Bloody Valentine covering 'Yesterday' by the Beatles," and then of course it would just be a regular version of "Yesterday" or a WAV file of a kid making armpit farts.

Once you had amassed a hard drive full of rare unreleased special rare rarities, you also ran the risk of losing your record collection. It wasn't a matter of somebody breaking into your car anymore; an errant click could destroy it all. My roommate, who didn't have a computer and who still checks his e-mail about once a year, was responsible for downloading a virus to my computer one day, and I was absolutely traumatized. Was I going to lose all those unreleased Weezer songs I worked so hard to acquire? I spent all weekend carefully reassembling playlists, reorganizing folders, and making sure I had up-to-date virus software. The hours I spent downloading music in college, the hours I did not spend outdoors or doing my sociology homework, came to nothing, in the end, because all that music disappeared when the computer I'd bought my freshman year broke down five years later.

You are always going to lose your record collection. Ask my dad, whose jazz records were destroyed when the basement flooded or were borrowed and never returned by his children. Ask my high school girlfriend, who left a box of cassettes at home when she left for college with a slim wallet of CDs. Ask me—the CD collection I spent fifteen years building with obsessive love and determination now exists in limbo, in two places simultaneously: the discs themselves are in cardboard boxes in the basement, and their digital ghosts are encoded on a lump of plastic and silicon the shape and size of a hardcover Bible.

When a new album I'm interested in comes out, I don't even buy it—I use the Internet to listen to it on someone else's computer, on a site like Pandora or eMusic. If you've got a little money to pay for subscription services like Rhapsody, or even Napster, which went legit, you can share the biggest record collection in the world. Music belongs to everyone. Or it belongs to no one. People now talk about the Internet as a "cloud," and if that is where our music is, we can finally face what was always the truth: you cannot catch and keep a sound.

FIVE ALBUMS (OR FOLDERS CONTAINING MP3 FILES) OF THE EARLY INTERNET AGE

 Radiohead, *Kid A* (Capitol, 2000)

This might have been where the paths diverged, and we started along the digital one we're on now, because I have two distinct memories of the "first time" I heard *Kid A*. One is of getting out of class on October 3, 2000, taking the bus to Sonic Boom Records in Seattle, buying *Kid A* there, and taking it back to my dorm room, where the opening notes of "Everything in Its Right Place" blew my mind. The other memory is of driving over to Daniel's house during the summer of that same year so he could play me the *Kid A* song "Treefingers," which he had just gotten off the Internet. It was about five minutes of arrhythmic drum banging that sounded like it had been recorded in an electrical storm. "Wow," I said. "I guess this album really is going to be weird." Daniel went on about how excited he was to hear the album and how experimental it was clearly going to be. And of course, in October, when I actually heard the smooth keyboard ambiance of "Treefingers," I realized that what I had heard on Daniel's computer had not been Radiohead at all—it was just some joker banging on sheet metal. *Kid A* is a beautiful album, and it says something about the possibility for real honest human warmth even in the face of the cold, unfeeling economy of technology. It also taught me that on the Internet, everybody is lying.

 ## Johnny Q. Public, *Extra*Ordinary* (Gotee, 1995)

This is (barely) a pre-Internet record, which I heard not because of a MySpace page, but because the band played a free show at a Christian bookstore in Spokane. They played outside in the parking lot, and I had never been that close to a band before. When I started being able to get on the Internet, I looked for info about this band but rarely found any, which is kind of the way I like it—there remains a mystery to them. *Extra*Ordinary* seems like straight-up grunge—the singer, Dan Fritz, has a classic gravelly wail—but there were little classic-rock tics that made it weird and great: the way they interpolated the brain pounding riff from Camper Van Beethoven's "Pictures of Matchstick Men" into the middle of "Body Be"; the covers of Larry Norman and Bob Dylan; the weird song based on an obscure Bible passage about women who lose their hair; the secret "track zero" (you had to rewind) version of "Father Abraham"; the sheer guttural emotion of "As I Pray" and "Black Ice"; and the spooky ballad "Big Top," with its terrifying mixture of cutesy glockenspiels and Calvinism. You can order *Extra*Ordinary* on Amazon.com for the sum of fourteen cents, so you really have no excuse not to, but you should also check out the records by Flick, a band that Johnny Q. Public guitarist Oran Thornton (who also played lead guitar on dc Talk's "Jesus Freak" single) was in for a few years in the early 2000s.

Weezer, *Weezer* (aka Green Album; Geffen, 2001)

Surprisingly, I haven't written a book about Weezer. This band, whose first two records have dominated my musical imagination for years, has now so negatively impacted their legacy with so many acts of sheer arena rock buffoonery that I am beginning to wish they had never existed at all, even if that means the world never got to hear *Pinkerton*. The *Green Album* was Weezer's comeback record, their breaking of the five-year silence after the brilliant and misunderstood *Pinkerton*, and when it leaked onto the Internet, I was faced with a dilemma: did I want to get a hold of the new album by my favorite band as quickly as possible or stay true to the Old Code of official release dates and Christmas Day–like excitement? A kid on the campus computer network had made available a tantalizing folder called "Weezer (2001)," so I caved. The record company also sent me two copies of it in advance for some reason, and if all that wasn't enough to destroy the mystique of the new album, it wasn't very good. "Island in the Sun" is a great single, and some of the melodies are truly excellent, but the lack of emotional investment from the band made for a huge anticlimax. I spent roughly five hundred hours of my life from 1999 to 2001 downloading scores of rare, unreleased songs by Weezer,[8] and I have nothing to show for it but my disappointment.

My Bloody Valentine, *Loveless* (Sire, 1991)

When Weezer emerged from five years of silence, they swung to the opposite extreme, releasing every inconsequential piece of information about their band via the Web. Another band I discovered during this era, My Bloody Valentine,[9] was the opposite of Weezer in every way—guitars a thousand layers thick and deep, with faraway, unintelligible vocals, a miasma of mystery with no Web site at all. I didn't even know what they looked like. The only source for information on MBV's lyrics, which I was intensely cu-

---

8. Mostly these songs were recorded circa 1992–98. And in case you're wondering, "Blast Off!," which was later released on the album *Alone: The Home Recordings of Rivers Cuomo*, is in fact the zenith of Cuomo's songwriting.

9. Whose record I bought, by the way, because Jason Martin from Starflyer 59 mentioned them in an interview.

rious about, was a fan-run Web site with a disclaimer that nobody really had any idea what the lyrics to any of their songs were. It turned out that all their songs were about sex, which I was a little shocked to learn. I later found out that *Loveless* is a Record You're Supposed to Like, and in an act of reverse psychology, I now find it difficult to listen to all the way through. I might actually like their previous album, *Isn't Anything*, better if it weren't for the punishing beauty of "Only Shallow." MBV have been threatening to finish a follow-up to *Loveless* for fourteen years and reunited for a spate of shows in the later part of the 2000s, but I can't imagine anyone will have patience for another record like this in an era of beat-driven, instantly downloaded singles.

 Björk, *Homogenic* (One Little Indian, 1997)

The first time I downloaded the Björk classic "All Is Full of Love," it was a live cover version by Death Cab for Cutie; I didn't hear Björk's version until much later, and the Björk album is a gorgeous piece of electronic-organic loveliness, but my questions is this: *Is* all full of love? I could see trees and flowers and puppies, but what about, I don't know, Kim Jong-Il and oil spills? Are they "full of love"? Oh, Björk, you know I'm just playing devil's advocate, you adorable pagan pixie. The thing is, when I am listening to that song and others like it on this album (especially the gorgeous "Jóga"), when I am completely covered and wrapped in it, I absolutely believe you. When the record is over, maybe I don't go back to my real life thinking that everything I encounter has behind it a driving force of goodness and light—there is too much darkness in this world for that to be true—but I do remember that while not everything is good, everything was created to be good, infused by the love of a Creator who maybe didn't have in mind that eventually we were going to waste all this love by frittering it away, spending days downloading songs in dark basements instead of interacting with the people he put here for us to love and to love us.

6

Faith and Doubt in the Shalom Zone

When you are young, you think the best thing you could possibly do is meet a musician whose music you really care about. He or she will be the One Who Really Gets You, and vice versa. You will probably hug and become pen pals, and maybe your favorite singer will take you on as an apprentice and produce your first album and you will become famous.

That never happens. I can count on one finger the number of my favorite songwriters whom I have hugged. We did not become friends, and it did not make me famous. In fact, things usually turn out much worse: I have had some supremely disappointing encounters with favorite musicians, who sometimes reveal themselves to be jerks or incoherent alcoholics. So I do not recommend that you do something I did when I met my favorite Christian rock band in 1996.

I was in the autograph line, effusive with compliments, telling the band how much I liked their show and their new record. I made one of these giddy fanboy comments to the bass player, who didn't seem to hear me. The following exchange took place:

Bass player (*quietly*): Sorry, I didn't hear you. I'm zoning.
Me (*not hearing or understanding*): What?
Bass player (*louder but unintelligible*): I'm *zoning.*
 Me: Huh?
Bass player: I'm ZO-NING.

Me: Sorry?

Bass player: *I HAVE A COLD, AND I'M ZONING.*

I took my autographed poster and went home. The bass player would spend the evening facing a long line of earnest Christian fans, and I would spend the evening replaying the incident in my head and wanting to die.

The act of getting an autograph is patently absurd, especially when you're getting an autograph from a dude who is only a few years older than you and the only difference between the two of you is that you play guitar at your youth group and he plays guitar at his youth group *and* on a national tour of churches.

That same year, I got an autograph from another guy in a band I loved, and the scene was again awkward. I walked up to the singer trying to think of something clever to say, anything to avoid a repeat of the "zoning" incident.

"Hey there, heh heh," I said, holding up a glossy photo of the band, attempting to obscure the obvious fact that I was the kind of person who would *purchase* a *photograph* of another human being and ask him to autograph it. "Can you write your name on this?"

He obliged, and the photo, with the singer's name not signed, but carefully printed in block letters, joined the Christian rock memorabilia on my bedroom wall.

Somehow, I guess, this experience was not enough for me, and so about eight years later I did something even more dangerous than asking for an autograph—I called him up to do an interview. Brian McSweeney had been the singer and guitarist for Seven Day Jesus, who were not a famous band, but whose music had meant a lot to me for years. To make a somewhat twisted analogy: did you ever hear Jeff Buckley say that Nusrat Fateh Ali Khan was his Elvis? To Buckley, this qawwali singer from Pakistan, unknown to most people who don't do yoga or buy Putumayo albums, was tantamount to the King, the biggest pop icon of the twentieth century. With that in mind, I recall McSweeney's enthusiasm for Buckley in an interview he did with a Christian music magazine. You can tell that McSweeney's crazy about Buckley and is falling all over himself to educate the interviewer. So if Khan was Buckley's Elvis, and Buckley was McSweeney's Khan, then maybe I can say McSweeney was my Buckley.[1] What I mean is: the kind of music that is played with guitars and drums is really important to me, and at any given time there are only a handful of people whose voices, chords, hooks, and lyrics fill me with an intangible gladness. And this guy was one of them.

The concert space at the Central United Methodist church was called the Shalom Zone. Daniel (who isn't named for the prophet of the Lion's den, but the Elton John song) and I made merciless fun of the Shalom Zone, mostly because we didn't know what it meant and thought it was stupid—"Dude, we're in the *Shalom Zone*!" It was another one of those insufferable Christiany things that I put up with and he didn't, or rather he did, because I dragged him to these things despite the fact that he was a lapsed Catholic who put about as much stock in religion as he did in returning rental videos on time—which is to say, not much.

But there we were at a Christian concert. I was conscious once again, as almost always, that this was a world I did not belong in, not really, and yet it was a world I loved and needed. I lacked the cheerleading enthusiasm of some of its denizens and the sheer social misfitry, the safety pins and punk rock patches, of some of the others. I was a kid who liked rock & roll, wearing a blue T-shirt with no slogans or logos on it, no "Jesus Is the Way," no Dead Kennedys button.

You are smart, of course, and you realize that the place was called the Shalom Zone, that we *did* belong there, that everyone belonged there, that Shalom is the peace and love and acceptance offered to humanity by God himself. At age fifteen, I didn't get that, not yet, so instead I made fun of everything.

In the crowd, there was a middle-aged man with a mustache, a leather jacket, and a green Mohawk, a curiosity of Christian culture. My guess is he was in a "motorcycle ministry" of some kind, but he could have just been a weirdo.

1. Or at least one of my top ten Buckleys; Buckley himself is also in the top ten, which makes this more than a little confusing.

"Rock for the Flock!" he shouted to no one in particular, right fist raised. "Jam for the Lamb!"[2]

"Biker or punk," said Daniel, "you can choose one, but not both."

Before the show, a pastor got up to pray. He talked about things that were not part of my vocabulary or consciousness, things like "the city" and "homeless youth." I didn't really know there were "homeless youth" in Spokane; to me, "the city" was not a place where people suffered and went without food and shelter. It was my house, my high school, the video store, concert venues, and Mexican fast food restaurants.

The pastor started to pray, thanking God for the venue, asking him to bless the bands who had traveled so far to share their music with us. To a Christian rock outsider, it must have looked ridiculous,[3] but we were used to this sort of thing. We did it all the time. Then the prayer changed direction a little and started to sound like something that was not even a prayer any more: "We've got kids who are dropping their pants for ten dollars," the pastor said. "But what really pisses me off is the people who are doing that shit, paying little kids to drop their pants."

This was confusing—does swearing about child exploitation count as a prayer?—but it felt like a jolt of reality. Sometimes at these concerts, the audience would start a cheer: "We love Jesus, yes, we do / We love Jesus, how 'bout you?" Then another section of the crowd would respond in turn, just like at a high school football game. The conclusion to the football cheer ("We've got spirit, yes, we do!") is supposed to end in a frenzy of "We got more! Hey! We got more! Hey!" This could not be more inappropriate for Christians, I thought. It was an orgy of one-upmanship, a taunting "we got more" to the world. I never cheered at football games or for Jesus. At that moment, though, this pastor seemed so unconcerned with who loved Jesus more. He was more concerned with who loved homeless kids and prostitutes.

A band called Seven Day Jesus took the stage before the band we had come to see, Black Eyed Sceva. We knew about Black Eyed Sceva because I had read about them in one of my Christian music

2. He really did say this.
3. I actually think it's kind of nice.

magazines. Their name was based on an obscure passage from the book of Acts in which a man possessed by an evil spirit beats up the seven sons of a priest, leaving them "naked and bleeding." They were a good band, but that was not something I could relate to.

Seven Day Jesus explained that their name means following Christ is something that you shouldn't just do on Sunday, but every day. I liked that. Something else I liked was that they didn't say anything else after that—no altar calls, no "We love Jesus, yes, we do." They just played the hell out of their set.

Seven Day Jesus played beautiful rock & roll, an especially tender version of that loud-quiet-loud style that was popular in that musical epoch, and their singer's voice had a remarkable clarity and purity. He almost sounded like the singer Daniel's guitar teacher[4] had told us about, Jeff Buckley. His voice was high and it is soared above the room like a bird. If I had heard of Marvin Gaye or Al Green, I would have been reminded of them. But I was not reminded of anything. This was a new world.

What happened next was even more confusing and exciting than the prayer: mid-song, the band was suddenly quiet. For a moment the silence was absolute, that glorious, brief moment that can never last at a concert—if the pause is more than half a second, someone will shout "Woo!" and the moment will be lost. For that brief moment, the world was standing still. We were frozen and rapt.

Seven Day Jesus only made two albums. Their first, *The Hunger*, had not been released yet when I first saw them play. It is a magnificent record, made with a fervor for God and rock & roll. I want to consider

4 You may be interested to know that the teacher was Myles Kennedy, who played in a band called the Mayfield Four before he joined the remnants of the band Creed to form Alter Bridge, before Creed got back together. I have very little to say about Creed (who a lot of people think are an important band in the history of Christianity and rock), because I think Scott Stapp is an awful singer and lyricist, but I will admit that I did once sing along to the song "Higher" in my car. And it felt like a spiritual experience, which I would like to deny, because Creed's guitarist always has this look on his face that communicates the message, "THIS RIFF I AM PLAYING IS TAKING EVERY OUNCE OF STRENGTH AND BODILY CONCENTRATON I CAN MUSTER AND IS THE MOST POWERFUL AND MEANINGFUL ROCKAGE EVER ROCKED," even though what he is playing sounds like this: "weedle-deeee-duh-lee-dooo."

their second album, *Seven Day Jesus*, a mistake, in the way that some people want to call REM's *Monster* or U2's *Pop* a mistake. I can't do this, though, because despite the album's production by a meddling Christian label that insisted on adding more references to God and Jesus, and despite McSweeney's admission that he'd been a little too enamored of the power pop of the Posies, the songs are still solid. His voice is still so sweet and so clear I want to believe him when he sings what sound like Sunday school clichés. It's all so beautiful, so well crafted and perfect, that it almost makes me sick when I listen to it now. Even though I know it was on Christian-major-record-label steroids, I love the simple faith in the lyrics, the joyful melodies.

I know things got more complicated after that and that no-body can go back to something that simple. Having left Christian music and done some time in an indie rock band called Lackluster, McSweeney put together a band called Matthew. Despite the biblical name, Matthew was nothing near a Christian band, and they did their best to steer the discourse on their Web site away from CCM. Matthew got a sweet deal with RykoDisc (only to lose it after the label was unhappy with sales) and wide enough distribution that I was able to find the record in the British city of Bath, where I was living the day it came out. It had taken eight years, but the Matthew album, *Everybody Down*, is the true ideological follow-up to *The Hunger*. The albums are both about surrender—*The Hunger* is a surrender to faith, *Everybody Down* is a surrender to doubt.

Something I am starting to realize: faith and doubt are not nec-essarily two sides of the same thing as much as they simply *are* the same thing. Some people might call unsure faith "being agnostic" or just confused, but that's the point of faith, right? Otherwise, we'd call it certainty. When I pick up books about "new atheism" or see blog screeds decrying how blind religious faith is destroying the human race, I can only sigh. These people, they are so *sure* about so many things, and they seem to think evangelicals are just as sure as they are, that we are crazy because we think we have it all figured out. But I think that's wrong. Not all of us think that we have it all figured out. I am not sure of a whole lot, because our faith is a mystery—that's in the Bible, for real—and mystery is confusing. We believe that there is a God and God loves us and Jesus showed us how to live and love each other. There are a lot of details that don't invite easy under-standing. I don't *like* being sure about facts, and we do not live in a world where rational scientific inquiry explains everything anymore. We are post-post-Enlightenment, and we live in a perpetually spreading gray area. I think God is here, too.

Everybody Down is a map of the gray area, and its high point, "Where Did You Go," a lilting ballad that becomes a soaring and desperate prayer, seems to reach for answers. But it doesn't find Bible verses or easy comfort. Instead, there are subtle references to faith, hope, and love, pulled off with more grace and maturity than any-thing a band recording for the Christian record industry could hope to achieve. *Everybody Down* is, ironically, about *the hunger* for a faith that had been all but lost somewhere among the record executives and Christian teenagers asking for autographs.

A few years after *Everybody Down* came out, I found myself on the phone with McSweeney. "The only reason I even call myself a Christian anymore is the fear of not being one," he said. "What kind of a reason is that? That's no reason."

I sat there half stunned, trying to figure out what to say next. I was in the middle of an essay for a literary journal, an essay about people "of faith" who make pop music. I was trying to track down my favorite bands to talk about creativity, spirituality, and rock music. The essay wasn't supposed to be about Christian music, but somehow what we ended up talking about was how he got screwed over by the Christian industry. He stopped talking to me for a min-ute, buying, I imagine, a pack of cigarettes at a convenience store in downtown Chicago. "To me, God is Truth," he said. "That's my god, the truth."

God is Truth. Truth is God. I had nothing to say, other than remem-bering to stammer that *The Hunger* had meant a lot to me and some of my friends, that it was one of the few records from the Christian rock era I still listened to almost ten years later. When he hung up, I felt aw-ful. Why did I get an empty ache in my stomach when someone I met once when I was sixteen voiced the same doubts that have plagued me? Is this how people felt when Amy Grant got divorced?

I sat back in my chair and looked around the borrowed office on the campus of a Christian college, looked out into the perfectly manicured lawn and felt the fluorescent lights boring into my eyes, giving me a splitting headache. I had been looking for someone to reassure me about the Big Questions that were starting to keep me awake, that made me cry like an infant surrounded by hipsters at the Crocodile Café when Pedro the Lion played their lack-of-faith lament "Secret of the Easy Yoke."

After a few minutes, an impossibly skinny, bleary-eyed guy named Noah knocked on the door. This wasn't a biblically symbolic *deus ex machina*—we had an appointment for an interview. Noah was a fragile person who sometimes sat silently for a minute or two before answering a question. He was a member of a symphonic, psychedelic rock band I admired for its seamless blending of artistry and religious imagery. He was also a member of a much more popular dance rock band that was about to leave on a national tour. He told me that music was divine, a gift from God—even the dance music that he sang into a computer that made his voice sound like a robot. He told me that he can't always pin a name on his faith, can't put a finger on the God that pushes him toward music. He told me that the best music is made by people who are, in some sense, believers, that it cannot really be made by anyone else.

Something drives Noah to sing into a machine, to travel the country in a van, to pile up empty bottles in every city, to sleep on sticky floors and wear sparkly shirts that read "LOVE," to play violin at a Presbyterian church on Sundays. It is the same thing, I think, that drives me to buy records about God and listen to them over and over, to stay up late searching for adjectives for album reviews, to figure out the bass lines to hymns.

When Noah left, I still had the headache, but we'd spent 120 minutes talking about how God and music and love are all that make life worth living, and how it is so damn hard to care so much about them when nobody else seems to, but that we can and must. That, to me, was truth.

The guitar feedback hung in the air. A drop of sweat fell from the singer's nose. And then he screamed, "Because you, you RAPE MY SOUL!"

I had never heard anything like this. The band played a distorted interval that cut into me, stabbing in a way the best music always does.

"RAPE MY SOUL! RAPE MY SOUL!"

My heart cracked open.

I didn't know exactly what McSweeney meant by those three words. Later I read that he'd written the song as a way to wrestle with the idea of forgiving a person who had raped a close friend, but in the years since the Shalom Zone, when I've listened to that song ("Forgive You"), I've never come to a definitive conclusion about its meaning. Sometimes I think the song is about how unforgivable something like that seems, and how to be truly Christlike we have to forgive the people who do to us the most egregious wrongs imaginable, and how impossible that feels. Other times I think about the shocking literary image from John Donne, who wrote "Batter My Heart, Three-Personed God," a poem asking God to destroy him in order to bring about rebirth and redemption, a poem in which he describes being "ravaged" by the Holy Spirit. I also think about the way people can be violated by churches and other Christians, their souls torn away by people who are supposed to bring healing but do not. "Rape my soul" is such a brutal, visceral, personal lyric, such a consummation of earthly violence and spiritual angst, a cry of faith and doubt.

But none of this was on my mind that night; I only knew that something new was beginning, that reality was becoming deeper and more complex and beautiful because of what was happening in that church basement. I knew that there was a God and that he in his mercy created electric guitars.

FIVE ALBUMS TO BOLSTER A SHAKY FAITH

 Seven Day Jesus, *The Hunger* (5 Minute Walk, 1996)

This album is not cutesy or cloying like so much of the music marketed to Christian teenagers. The band members were very young themselves when they made it, but there's a wisdom to the music and lyrics that makes the record immediately compelling. In "Forgive Me," the protagonist calls himself lower than Judas, and the liner notes explain that the title song confesses that faith in God is "unexplainable"—just to use that word in the evangelical world is a risk! This deep longing is everywhere on the record, from the soaring vocals and guitar lines to the wide-eyed soul searching. There is one lyric (only one) on *The Hunger* that rubs the wrong way. "Delightful You" asks a seemingly heretical question about God's paralysis by human inaction. The singer comes to the conclusion, though, that he must banish all doubt, cold turkey. The bridge repeats this as a mantra: "Just kill the doubt." It rings hollow on an album full of questions, and I have to wonder how McSweeney felt when he wrote that. Did he believe that killing doubt was that easy? Even when I was rocking out to this record in my bedroom, I knew it wasn't.

Pedro the Lion, *It's Hard to Find a Friend* (Made in Mexico/ Jade Tree, 1998)

It's Hard to Find a Friend was kind of *the* record when I was in college, the one where everything and everyone came together. It wasn't the record for the kids at chapel with frosted blonde hair whose pictures were in the school's recruitment brochure; it was the record for the people I knew, the ones who skipped chapel, smoked cigarettes, took too many diet pills, wrote sex poems, played in bands, read Kerouac, and hungered for communion with God. David Bazan's lovely, simple indie rock songs—songs that were carried forward by plaintive vocals and subtly twisting bass lines—were about things that really mattered to us. While dc Talk was singing songs like "Hey You (I'm into Jesus)," Bazan was singing about regular-person stuff, the difficulties of just being a youngish American Christian dude. It was his song "Secret of the Easy Yoke" that really got us, a song about wanting to want to love God, wanting to want to follow Jesus, but just not getting it and sometimes not wanting it and not understanding it, while holding out hope for that "still, small voice" we'd heard our theology professors mention. It was a prayer for the mix of awesome power and blessed assurance Jesus showed the disciples when he said to the storm, "Peace, be still." Bazan's struggle with faith has since played out rather publicly on his most recent record, *Curse Your Branches*, which nearly eighty-sixes faith altogether while leaving the door open a crack for that voice. Almost everyone I knew in college held *It's Hard to Find a Friend* dear. We didn't just love it, we lived it.

Jeff Buckley, *Grace* (Columbia, 1994)

Let me first state that Jeff Buckley's legacy has been almost entirely destroyed by the spate of useless material released under his name. He rivals Tupac Shakur in the size of his posthumous discography, nearly all of it live versions of songs from *Grace*. You always think they have run out of in-studio radio-session versions of "Last Goodbye," yet Columbia always has another collection of them to release next year. This is not cool, because *Grace* is probably the most visceral, beautiful rock record released in my lifetime. From Buckley's tortured groan and the spastic guitar triplets on "Mojo Pin" to the vaguely qawwali groove and meditation on Buckley's loss of his father on "Dream Brother," listening to *Grace* is an emotionally draining experience. At first, I was skeptical—*just one dude on the cover, is this a singer-songwriter record? I am into punk bands.* But when I started looking at some of the song titles ("Corpus Christi Carol," "Grace," "Eternal Life") and then listened to them, I was won over by the mixture of the sensual and the spiritual. There is no mention of God anywhere on the record, strictly speaking, but there is an earthy sense of belief in every lyric and vocal cadence. *Grace* is the sound of a man making music with all his heart and mind and strength, and though I would not have wanted to see this as a worthy goal when I was seventeen, *Grace* is an absolute wonder to behold.

Wonderful, *God Bless Our Pad* (self-released, 2003)

These are actually the same people responsible for the band United State of Electronica, and the impulse (love, love, love!) is the same, though the music isn't. Named after a Brian Wilson composition (they copped some of his lyrics on their debut EP, *Welcome to Wonderful*), Wonderful is kind of a Beach Boys without the California—more autumn leaves. There are some songs about losing and joy, but the whole thing just feels like one blob of a set piece. Wonderful is not a religious band in a proselytizing sense, like most of my favorite Christians bands, but they are in the sense that the world of this record is clearly presided over by what they call "the God above." Synths swell and soar with the power of an orchestra, and the delicate vocals belie the power at work here, finally culminating in the epic "The Beach," which can't be about much other than God: God as ocean, as all-sustaining life force, declaring "with every wave I show my love for you."

 Spiritualized, *Let It Come Down* (Arista, 2001)

Apparently, Jason Pierce can make albums like *Let it Come Down*, with songs like "Lord Can You Hear Me," without believing in God. He's said in interviews that he has no religious feelings, that he just uses the iconography. Perhaps for Pierce they are empty symbols or ideas with no tangible real-world corollaries. Perhaps for him God just means love or transcendence or joy or happiness. I guess God means all those things, but God also refers to a particular reality, an ultimate thing who is there, who is alive, and who somehow helps us out and will welcome us to him someday. I'm ok with using "Lord Can you Hear Me" as a faith song, even if Pierce only uses it as a musical idea. Because it gets at a question that is very near to my heart: Can God hear me? And if I use a song, will he hear me better? Will he like what he hears? Will he be pleased by that secret chord, to paraphrase Leonard Cohen? I don't know the answers, but I find myself in the questions Spiritualized asks in these chaotic guitar gospel songs.

7

Anyone Can Play Guitar

I'M WITH THE BAND

In 2003, I interviewed Ben Gibbard and Chris Walla from Death Cab for Cutie at a coffee shop in downtown Seattle. This was while they were still only indie-famous (right before *Transatlanticism* came out) and were just starting to get regular-famous. It was pretty exciting because the last time I had been assigned to do a feature on Death Cab, they had fobbed me off with a drummer interview. I can say this with some degree of self-deprecation as a drummer myself: interviewing a drummer is like finding out you won a raffle where the first prize was, like, a trip to the Bahamas, but you got the second prize, which was a case of Twix bars from Costco. It's still cool—I really like Twix a lot—but the drummer is just a guy you have to have in order to be a band. He doesn't (usually) write the songs and he doesn't (usually) have anything interesting to say. In fact, at that time, Death Cab hadn't had a regular drummer for very long, and he left the band soon afterward.

I was, then, a little giddy about my brush with indie-fame, though I had been interviewing bands long enough to remain mostly composed. Through the picture window of the café, I saw Gibbard walking down First Avenue, and he almost looked like a caricature of an indie rocker—giant earmuff-style headphones, messenger bag, eyes wide and head in the clouds like he was lost in his own private soundtrack to the world. He looked like the kind of guy who would probably be listening to the Postal Service if it weren't for the fact that he *was* the guy from the Postal Service.

The interview went well. I knew enough about the band not to ask stupid questions,[1] and I had a fine moment when my friend Brian, who I'd worked with at the college radio station, happened to be walking by and I casually introduced him to "Ben" and "Chris." They gave me some advice about what kind of drums to buy (which I did not follow, because I had no money), and we talked about a band we both liked (although I just liked their music; these guys were friends with them).

There was one stupid question I couldn't avoid, though, one that my mind sometimes leaps to whenever I am thinking about some piece of art or music that I really like, which is: Why? What drove someone to create this? Even if it's just a three-minute pop song, my teleology radar kicks in. Blame the theology and philosophy classes I had to take at Catholic high school and Christian college, but I want to know for what greater purpose Death Cab composed "The Sound of Settling." After mentioning that I was glad the interview had gone well and I hadn't asked any stupid questions like "Why do you play music?" I went for it.

"So, uh, so why do you play music? Ha ha," I asked, trying to pretend like it wasn't a question I was obsessed with and urgently wanted to know the answer to.

Gibbard looked at me with what I assume was mild disdain. "Well, why do you write about music?" he asked.

"Uh, because I like it," I replied.

"I think it's sort of the logical extension of anything that you love," replied Walla, deigning to give an actual answer to the question Gibbard and I were both skirting. It's an uncool answer, love, but it works. "If you love looking at photographs, you figure out how to make them," he continued. "If you love reading books, you figure out how to make those. That's my answer."

---

1. The two stupidest questions you can ask a band, in case you were wondering, are "Where'd you get your name?" and "What are your influences?"

I love reading books, but I also love listening to music. And I have tried to learn how to make both, to varying degrees of success.

Something odd: although I was thoroughly ensconced in the world of CCM during my musically formative years, I never quite managed to be in a Christian band. I sometimes thought I should, and even worried that not being in a Christian band made me "lukewarm," the kind of Christian who is "neither hot nor cold," which God refers to in the book of Revelation, the likes of whom he says he will puke out of his mouth.[2] I get a little freaked out whenever this comes up, like the time a cross-eyed unshaven man on rollerblades accosted me and some friends on the Tube in London during a study abroad trip.

"You're going to hell," he said, as my seatmates tried to ignore him.

"We're already Christians," I told him.

"Why are you not out telling your friends about Jesus?" he asked. "Their blood will be on your hands." Rather than intense and angry, he was nonchalant and almost jovial about this.

"Look, we go to a Christian school," I said. "We're just here to study."

I remembered the videos and plays I'd seen in youth group about a group of teenagers who tragically die, where half of the teens begin to ascend to heaven and the other half are unceremoniously carted off to hell.[3] "Why didn't you tell us about Jesus?" the hell-bound teens always complained. The guilt I felt after those skits could easily be assuaged if I played in a Christian band, I thought. I wouldn't even have to say anything embarrassing; I could just play the drums.

2. This is sort of gross, and it also begs the question about how and whether God could puke and what it would look like. Would it be some kind of perfect Divine Vomit? Maybe instead of bile and half-chewed-up hamburgers it would be, like, a Thanksgiving dinner. Or even worse, maybe it would be an entire river of disgusting stomach contents, a Nile of bile. These are things you have to consider.

3. My favorite was a church camp skit in which two recently deceased friends met in the afterlife.

Teen Girl 1: How'd you die?
Teen Girl 2: I overdosed, on . . . pot.

When I was a bit younger, it seemed, based on what I heard in church, that one of the main things about being a Christian was trying to get other people to become Christians (there is a precedent for this in the Bible, obviously, but it's a bit complicated), mostly by doing things like—as an acquaintance once put it—"increasing the amount of Jesus in every conversation."[4] I have never been very good at this in conversations or in songs. The first song I ever wrote was at my grandparents' manufactured home in Arizona. It was called "Field of Cows," and the chorus was "I don't know why / And I don't know how / But all I can say is we're driving through this field of cows." Spiritual insight beyond this (it does present a kind of existential dilemma, maybe) never really manifested in my songwriting. In later years, I stuck to the drums.

My first foray into "band" territory was when my friend Daniel and I decided that for our final project in junior high social studies class—the entire assignment was to "do a big project and turn it in at the end of the year"—we would write a song. We didn't know anything about songs other than that we liked them, and I had a guitar, which neither of us knew how to play. Eventually, I figured out a way to tune the guitar so that all you had to do was put your index finger across all six strings on one fret and you'd be playing a bar chord—no hands was E; the first fret, F; the second, F-sharp; and so on. We continued doing this for at least our first year of being a "band."

Although I had grown up in a household where my mother regularly played classical music on the piano and my father frequently quizzed me on whether Mozart or Handel was playing on the stereo, I had up until then assumed that that was how a guitar worked. I figured you moved your hand up and down the neck, and the chords sort of took care of themselves. Our other ingenious invention—because if you have not played the guitar before, it hurts your fingers to play—was using a capo, rather than a finger, to press down on all the strings at once, which meant that changing from one "chord" to another took several seconds. Our songs, therefore, were very slow and had roughly two chords. There were also no lyrics, because, as you know if you have ever been a thirteen-year-old male, we didn't have a lot of

---

4. I just googled "increase the amount of Jesus" to see if this is a stock phrase (apparently it isn't), and Google suggested that I might be looking for "increase the amount of sperm," which has a number of disturbing implications.

confidence in our voices. The song was awful, but we got an A on it (as did everyone else, including the kid who wrote, "HEY MR. MORGAN ARE YOU ACTUALLY READING THESE PAPERS OR DO YOU JUST PUT A GRADE ON THE LAST PAGE" in the middle of his essay).

This encouraged us, and thus Daniel and I embarked on a long and storied career of half-assed high school rock bands, under the various names Caesarhead, Hot Buttered Noodles, the Junkets, Strawberries Galore (my favorite, due to its absurd degree of uncoolness), and Mr. Sanders. Most of our songs, like the first, were made up on the spot. The lyrics came directly from books on my parents' shelves, like *Moby-Dick* and *Alice in Wonderland*. One particularly imaginative ditty took its verses from a book called *The Children's Almanac of World Facts* and its chorus from the novel *Kim* by Rudyard Kipling, which, if you think about it, could have been a great commentary on postcolonial globalization. We never bothered to finish the lyrics to any of our original songs because we figured we could just make something up at our shows. I can't recommend this—an epic trip-hop jam, "Adam's Heart Stopped," was supposed to be about a friend who'd had a brush with death, but it ended up with only four lines ("This song is about a kid / who had a heart attack / I think he fell down / and hurt his back") followed by three minutes of pointless interplay between tom-toms and wah-wah pedal.

During high school, we averaged about two songs and one concert per year. The pursuit that took up most of our time as a band was being awesome. We spent most of our time thinking up new names for the band, talking about what we would wear if we ever played a show (Daniel splurged on a Hugh Hefner–style smoking jacket for the first such occasion), creating elaborate scenarios for theatrical stage shows that we never actually carried out ("We'll throw candy at the audience!" "We'll transition into a Radiohead cover, then just let the song devolve into total chaos and smash our guitars!"), and, very rarely, playing music. During my senior year, that band fizzled out, mostly because we couldn't keep other members longer than a few months, and I joined two new bands: one was a piano-pop band in the style of Ben Folds Five, called Persona Non Grata; the other was the Boxcar Children, a pop-punk band in the style of the Foo Fighters and Green Day. The Boxcar Children, who luckily never got famous, because there would have been a trademark dispute with another band of the same name, were originally called Norml. The joke was that we weren't *normal* because we were spelling *normal* in an *abnormal* way (get it?). After we'd printed T-shirts, someone pointed out that NORML was the name of a marijuana legalization advocacy group.

The lyrics in these bands were better, in the sense that they were written ahead of time, and although the songs were yearningly earnest (yearnest?) in the way that matters to teenagers, they were not Christian bands, except maybe for the fact that all the members were Catholic school attendees. The closest we got to CCM was a Boxcar Children lyric about "the path to the wrong way," which recalls church camp testimonies of "hanging out with the wrong crowd" and then eventually seeing the light. Sometimes I would play Persona Non Grata songs for the Boxcar Children guys while they listened politely, and vice versa, and then my bandmates would accuse the other group of being Christian. I guess I was just the kind of guy who seemed like he'd be in a Christian band.

That was the year that both of my bands made it into the downtown Spokane Battle of the Bands, a city-sponsored event for high school musicians that went by the puzzling name BOBFest. This was a goal I'd been working toward for my entire teenage life, and it was sweet. Even though my name was spelled wrong in the newspaper, it was in there—twice—and my bands rocked the house. We drove our upright piano in the back of a pickup to the middle of the park and loaded it onto the stage, much to the annoyance of the sound guys. Daniel came up to play some crazy digital-delay guitar. Stephen stomped across the piano keys during the climax of the last Persona Non Grata song. In a rare fit of showmanship, I wore a giant green foam cowboy hat. Three girls from my school showed up wearing "Joel Hartse Fan Club" T-shirts. I was only eighteen, and all of my rock star dreams had been realized.

DIVINE DESTRUCTION

My main goals after high school were:
1. Move to Seattle.
2. Start a band.

I guess some other things were in there too, like "go to college" or "figure out what to do with my life," but what I mostly wanted to do with my life was be in a band in Seattle, so I figured I was good to go. There was another thing, too: I think I was ready to be in a Christian band of some kind, if only to prove to myself that such a thing was possible. I was overjoyed to find out, on the first day of school, that my new roommate, Nathan, was a piano player, and the guy who lived next door to us played guitar.

We started a band immediately, and since we all had fairly high-minded ideas about faith and art, we were *not* a Christian band. We were the kind of band that sometimes plays Christian venues and occasionally writes songs about God and whose members are all Christians and even listen to Christian music, but know they will lose credibility if they say, "We're a Christian band," and go as far out of their way as possible to avoid giving the impression of being associated with such things. In other words, we totally were a Christian band.

The only thing left to do was to find an obscure C. S. Lewis reference for our band's name. When that didn't pan out, we went with Flicker, which was based on a quote from some lesser C. S. Lewis-ish theologian, something about how the desires we feel as lovers are just flickers of God's love for us. That wouldn't have been so bad, really, except that a band on a popular reality show at the time had a similar name. We eventually went with the Dandelion Method, based on yet another quote from a Christian writer, Philip Yancey, who used that phrase to explain that "What Jesus brought to a few—healing, grace, the good-news message of God's love—the church can now bring to all."[5] It's a tall order, but we were tall guys.

The best way we knew to bring good news was via loud guitars, so we didn't become missionaries or aid workers in war zones. We became a rock band, practicing one to three nights a week for nearly five years. We played whenever possible, at cafés and dive bars and house shows and once, for seven hundred dollars, at a megachurch whose youth group spent forty-five minutes throwing pancakes at each other and at us. Was it worth it to forsake our homework and jobs and free time so we could be hit in the face by cold flapjacks or play to our girlfriends and five drunk people at one o'clock in the

5. Yancey, *The Jesus I Never Knew* (Grand Rapids: Zondervan, 1995), 228.

morning on a Monday night? Yes. Because once in a while, in a dank hole of a bar somewhere, something beautiful happened.

Cue *Wayne's World*–style flashback: doodle-eedle-oo, doodle-eedle-oo, doodle-eedle-oo . . .

"I'm going to be your new booking agent here and at a few clubs around town," says the man we now refer to as Slick. Slick is the kind of person who *aspires* to be a sleazy music industry insider but whose general vibe is that of a guy who works at Quiznos and has starred in a few low-budget pornographic films. The venue he represents, where our band is about to play, has a reputation for showcasing has-been rock bands and being inhospitable to local artists. He is our new best friend.

"How many spots can we get on the guest list?" I ask. I'm hoping our girlfriends will be able to get in free—it's only fair, since they come to every show, and there are only so many times you can listen to pop songs about spiritual angst before it turns boring.

"Let me tell you the good thing about not having a guest list," Slick replies. "See, this is a Battle of the Bands, so you win based on how many ticket buyers vote for you, so you want to have people paying to come to see you."

We are not here to win the Battle of the Crappy Bands Who Couldn't Get a Show Downtown. We're just here to play our rock & roll on a real stage in a place where they serve beer. It's almost time for us to start, but I notice that the first band hasn't even taken the stage. Also, the bands Slick told us we would be playing with aren't here. And the marquee outside advertises a third set of bands, who are also not here tonight. So far, so good.

We're sandwiched between a middle-aged metal band and a ten-piece hip-hop group of high school kids from the suburbs. We are going to earn about $20 tonight and not drink any free beer for fear that somebody reports our drinking to the authorities of our Christian university as a violation of the school's "lifestyle expectations." We will somehow allow Slick to convince us that coming back for another Battle of the Bands on another Monday night next month will be a good idea.

Our second show at Slick's esteemed venue is a night like most others. We're slated to play last, which I used to think would mean we were "headlining," but I now know means "nobody is going to come see us play after midnight on a weekday." The marquee simply reads "TONIGHT."

The first band, the Blue Men, is musically tight, and their singer is actually good, but the overall impression is one of sad, lonely men doing their best U2 impression, which, at an unpopular bar in a yuppie neighborhood, is just depressing. The next band, Polythene, is one of those pretentious electronic bands with about five drum machines and ten synthesizers that takes two hours to set up and sound check, and of course, they play their noodly, pointless jams for over an hour. I would be enjoying myself—I do kind of like that type of music—but I have a sinking suspicion that we aren't going to play at all tonight. There is no one left in the club but the promoter, the bartender, two girlfriends, and a man who wandered in off the street and passed out on a table. After some deliberation, we decide to play anyway. We're young and living the dream—what do we care that we're tired, irritable, and have exams tomorrow?

In fact, since we don't feel any obligation to play well, we are sounding great. Everything's coming together: Kevin's moody feedback harmonics are ringing out, Matt's homemade distortion pedal is working well for once. Nathan, our keyboardist, incites band and audience members to remove their shirts (dudes only—we're Christians), and in what is probably the highlight of the entire evening, the sound guy (with thick glasses and stringy black hair, he is creepy even by sound guy standards) walks up on stage shirtless, his white potbelly a beacon in the dim room.

Tonight, instead of ending our closing song on a gentle fade-out as usual, the Dandelion Method spontaneously breaks into a noise freak-out somewhere between Sonic Youth and prog metal. Matt and Kevin turn their guitars and effects up; screeches and squalls of feedback fill the room. I'm battering the drums, when I look up to see that Kevin has turned around and is in the process of knocking my drums over, and two things hit me: first, the sharp edge of a cymbal, squarely in the back of the head, and second, the realization that *I am in a rock band and we are trashing the stage. My life is complete.* I may be bleeding, but I continue to play, now on my knees. Kevin continues to kick pieces of the set over and throws down his microphone stand.

Incredibly, Andrew, who almost never even moves while playing the bass, kicks over a mic stand.

This is the kind of thing that I've been hoping to experience ever since I started my love affair with rock music. As a drummer, I inhabit a space between creation and annihilation; to play the drums is, in a way, to destroy them. The creative destruction of rock & roll has always seemed to me to have a kind of divine impulse to it—I agree with Bach that all music is for the glory of God, and I agree with the Bible that God is love, and I love music, and this orbit of God-music-love really comes alive when you are bashing away on the drums or throttling the hell out of a guitar. I used to go to shows and marvel at how much creative energy the bands were releasing, how dangerously aggressive it seemed, the sheer beauty of a band laboring to give birth to a song. And now I am doing it.

The noise continues to rage. All that's left standing are my floor tom and snare drum, and I'm pounding them furiously. I don't care that it's one thirty in the morning and that I have class in a few hours. We don't care that we got screwed by Slick and the other bands and that we aren't going to get any money or sell any records. We just want to destroy this stage because God is Love.

COME TOGETHER

Even though we loved music, there was something oppressive about Sunday afternoons in the basement where the Dandelion Method practiced. Over beers, when the tape wasn't rolling, interminable conversations (about purpose, aesthetics, the band's name—Nathan was convinced for a weekend that switching to "Elephants Gerald" would be a good move) threatened to derail all possibility and promise, and they sometimes gave me a kind of despair about my existence, because the truth was, I didn't have anything better to do with my life than to wonder if more reverb and cooler album artwork would get us a gig at the Showbox. This was my life: I sat behind my drums looking sullen, in my standard-issue indie rock uniform (vintage jacket, '70s flat-front pants, black Converse, gaunt torso), and picked inconsequential fights about rock music.

"Do you guys like singing?" Kevin asked during one of these existential sessions.

Yeah, we pretty much all agreed, we do like singing.

"I don't."

It was a signal that Kevin was going to be the first one to leave the band. Kevin was a great singer, with a fragile, lilting voice that only bloomed under the right circumstances, but when it did, it was glorious. We watched as Kevin's musical taste took him from hippie-ish acoustic pop to slow, monotonous post-rock to ambient, meandering noise pieces. It wasn't that we immediately became a ham-fisted pop-punk band when Kevin left—that took a few months—it was that even as we piled on the heartfelt lyrics and harmonies, we lost a sense of the grandiose. We still wrote long, weird, twisting instrumentals, but they weren't imbued with the gravity and mystery that his songs were, somehow.

After he left for Portland, Kevin joined some other bands and made his own post-rock record under the name Glowworm. The Kevin I'd gotten to know, the earnest kid who once played in an acoustic band called God's Own Fools, shrank into the shadow of the sounds he created. He stopped singing.

While we were playing together, we all disappeared into the music, in a way, and that is what makes playing in a band so supremely satisfying. A group of five becomes one body, and when that musical unity is achieved, it is divine.

To get two people to work well together in a romantic relationship is a miracle. To make an emotionally charged (because you are nineteen to twenty-five years old) five-way rock group run smoothly is simply impossible—a band like the Dandelion Method, with four singers and five songwriters, isn't even a democracy: it's anarchy. We were all in a phase of life when acquiring and listening to new songs was a daily right and necessity. We embraced and absorbed any and everything we were listening to, and we each were listening to wildly different things—indie rock from Seattle, obscure Brazilian ragtime pianists, experimental ambient noise, the campus worship team. In short, we were a mess. The only time a record of ours was reviewed, the writer dropped completely disparate band names as possible influences, none of which were accurate reflections of what we actually listened to: Polvo, the Beach Boys, King Crimson, Chick Correa.[6] "We sound like a mix tape," Kevin said. It wasn't even a cohesive mix tape. We were like iTunes on shuffle.

Our songs, taken together, did not sound like the output of one entity, but within the space of one song, we were gloriously one. The Dandelion Method was the sum of our desires, and not only the musical ones—into that band's music we poured our struggles with God, family, alcohol, pride, love, hope, and each other. Being the drummer in the Dandelion Method, as small and meaningless as the endeavor was, as little recognition and money[7] we received for playing once a month at the Lock and Keel Tavern, still stands as one of the most rewarding experiences of my life, if only for those tiny moments of musical communion.

Peter R. Scholtes,[8] once a Catholic priest, later a husband and father and management consultant, wrote a song called "They Will Know We Are Christians by Our Love," a fairly ubiquitous tune—maybe you sang it in your church. The last time I heard it mentioned was by a postmodern funk DJ in a cab ride in Shanghai. "They Will Know . . ." is one hell of an optimistic song, and it's also a challenge, for it doesn't tell us what we do, but what we *will* do—work side by side, walk hand in hand, love. And surely, the implication is that we will not do this alone, we could not do this alone, we must have help from the Spirit.

Since the band broke up, too many other things have gotten in the way of even allowing five people who used to play music together to be in the same physical space at the same time—moves cross-country, new girlfriends and breakups, PhDs, hospital stays, children, jobs—and so the line that really gets me in Scholtes's song is the one about how our unity will be restored. This idea of restoration, of things going back to the way they ought to be, is not just a part of how I think about my old band, but how I think about what I

6. I have at one time or another owned records by all of those bands, but you simply could not write a song that was influenced by those four artists. It would tear itself apart.

7. $100, which was spent entirely on post-show pizza for everyone who came to see us.

8. You might remember him as the Catholic folk-rocker from earlier in this book.

want from the world. I'm sure it has something to do with what the author of Ecclesiastes says about God setting eternity in our hearts.

The music I made with my friends, and the relationships, musical and otherwise, mean so much to me, though they have been eroded by the vagaries of time and geography. We are all singing new songs now, songs we didn't write together, and we'll probably never play music together again. That makes me sad, but it also reminds me of the only truly good lyric I ever came up with, for a Pixies rip-off that was the last song we ever recorded: "It might be over for now, but now is not forever."

FIVE RECORDINGS BY BANDS I WAS IN

 Ten Sleep Crow Agency, *Demo EP* (unreleased, 1995)

The average age of the members of this band (Daniel, who now works at a Santa Fe art gallery, on guitar; Parker, now a corporate executive in Silicon Valley, on drums; me, now writing this book in Vancouver, on bass) was fourteen and a half, and this, I think, is the reason it is so awesomely bad. Here is a recording of three dudes who really liked music but really had no idea about exactly what it was or how you made it. The band is named after two small towns in Montana we found on a map in my parents' basement, and the one original song on the demo, "He Eventually Caught the Porker," is essentially two-chord[9] punk/metal, a song whose lyrics we improvised by the ingenious method of "shout the name of a thing you see in this room." (Sample stanza: dun-nanunnanunnanunna dunnanunnanunnanunnanunna dun-nanunnanunnanunnanunna nuh! "Toothpaste!") The other two songs are Christian rock covers: "She's the Queen" by Starflyer 59, the last ten seconds of which are the only listenable music on the tape (Daniel's whammy-bar guitar solo meant he couldn't play chords, so your ears could rest after the three minutes of feedback sludge that preceded it); and "Last Breath" by PFR—both sung, in a slurring baritone, by me, through a pair of headphones dangling from a music stand.[10] I would pay actual money to hear this recording again.

9. F and F-sharp, obviously.

10. Headphones as a proxy for an actual piece of necessary music technology

The Boxcar Children, *Boxcar Children EP* (unreleased, 1999)

This EP was recorded in a studio that has shared its space with a metal foundry and a dental floss company, which ought to tell you something about how successful it was as a recording studio. Still, making a real live record was worth the three hundred dollars apiece we had to save up. We ripped through five songs without a click track, and my main contribution to this recording, other than playing the bass badly and singing falsetto backing vocals, was continually telling the engineer to "make it sound like Weezer." He actually did, and I consider that a success. I did not write any lyrics for this band, and although I'm not saying mine would've been better, the best line on the whole five-song EP is a verse from our song "Paper Airplane": "Once / in a town of many people / there was this kid who was a weasel / I kicked his ass / I kicked his ass / now that's not too hard to grasp." For most of the year that I was in this band, I strapped my bass guitar around my waist with an old belt and did not realize that if I wanted to tune it, I should put my ear up to the amplifier, which is where the sound comes from, and not the strings themselves like I did with my acoustic guitar. The quality of both my musical gear and knowledge has barely improved in the intervening ten years.

The Friskies, *Limp*Frizkies* (unreleased, 2000)

The band formerly known as Persona Non Grata changed its name, because we assumed no one would get the highbrow Latin. So naturally, we renamed our band for a popular brand of cat food, which I think was a good move. Our only approximation of an "album" is an eight-song set we recorded, mostly live, in my friend Stephen's parents' living room, where they had a grand piano.[11] More than any other record I have made, *Limp*Frizkies* is a mixture of absurd, awful, and brilliant. It contains a triptych of songs inspired by Stephen's job at a local bakery,[12] a funk jam

---

was a common theme for this band. At one gig a few years later, where we played a cover of Blur's "Song 2" to a room of grade school–aged children, we used a pair of headphones clamped to the body of an acoustic guitar in lieu of an electric. Also, Parker was unable to make it to the show, so we replaced him with an eleven-year-old kid we'd met earlier that day. Punk rock!

11. A pseudonym, because of the last two sentences in this paragraph and because "Stephen" is now a corporate lawyer.

12. The subject matter of which were, respectively, a mysterious rash he'd ac-

about making out with an unattractive girl, several overwrought spiritual epics, and a jazz waltz. Stephen later passed out after drinking an entire bottle of Wild Turkey, and, upon waking, he found he had lost the use of his right arm, which remained paralyzed for an entire year. At least we made this record first.

The Dandelion Method, *The Mystery, the Science, Unraveling* (self-released, 2002)

As much as I want this to be the first "real" or "good" or "cohesive" record I had a hand in making, it is not necessarily any of those things. *TMTSU* (as it is destined to be known by music scholars in the future) is the sound of five young men who are really excited about the idea of being in a band[13] but are not sure if that band is Phish, Weezer, Mogwai, Ben Folds Five, the Dave Matthews Band, or Switchfoot. It was a true DIY project in the sense of, like, "this is so poorly put together it's hard to believe it actually worked." We did a photo shoot for the liner notes at two o'clock in the morning on the day we released the album and spent the entire day printing copies of it in the campus computer lab before the show. This is the only record I have ever heard that contains both a Japanese spoken-word piece over scary Tim Burton–style circus music *and* a 6/8 punk-rock doo-wop breakup song. This album is available somewhere on the Internet, and I hope you do not look for it.

Biltus, *Just Us and Us EP* (self-released, 2005)

After the Dandelion Method broke up (five years and two slightly less uneven recordings later), Matt and Andrew and I stuck around for a few months in Seattle to make this record. With only three people making decisions, things were a lot easier, and the record came together with ease. The Biltus[14] record is pure power pop without all the pesky music-major things the other dudes who

---

quired on the job, the disappearance of the rash, and an elaborate false scenario involving important government documents and baked goods.

13. This is a common theme in my musical history, much more common than themes like practicing hard in order to get really good at an instrument or knowing how to read music.

14. The band is named for a misunderstanding about the band Built to Spill. My fried Matt's wife thought he really liked a band called "Biltus Bill," which we loved so much that we decided to use it. I still kind of feel bad about naming our band this. We weren't making fun of you, Jacinda, honest!

moved away added to the band, like minor sevenths and intel-
lectually stimulating melodies. It consists of big dumb songs with
four chords, and it sounds great. In an alternate-universe version
of my life, Biltus is a successful indie rock band touring the country. In real life, we played three shows at which I drank an average
of one pitcher of beer per show. It was a good run.

8

I Spent $100,000 on College and All I Got Was This Radio Station

ANOTHER DRAMATIC CONVERSION NARRATIVE INVOLVING A SKA BAND

The less said about college, the better. It is a time in one's life only slightly less embarrassing, in retrospect, than junior high, except the braces and inopportune boners are replaced by Bob Marley posters and puking in garbage cans. Unless, of course, you go to a Christian school, in which case they are replaced by Caedmon's Call records and sexually charged Bible studies. I am a graduate of such a university, but I feel I should qualify the term *Christian university* for those who might not come from the world I do. Christianity, as you may know, is a very popular world religion that has been around for roughly two thousand years. It has many different expressions and groups of people who understand it in certain differing ways, and some of these people run universities. (Church history lesson finished.)

There are many different kinds of Christian universities: you have the Catholic ones, like Notre Dame, Georgetown, or Boston College, which tend to be similar to regular universities except that you sometimes see a priest walk by and there is a cathedral on campus. You have private liberal arts colleges that were started by certain Christian groups but which are now religious by tradition only; these are small and expensive and snooty. You have the super-conservative, unaccredited, slightly insane schools where rock & roll music and physical contact between opposite genders are prohibited. And finally, you have the traditionally evangelical private liberal arts universities, which are relatively normal but where everybody is eerily well-dressed, good-looking, and holy, and which are part of something called the Council for Christian Colleges and Universities.

It's at a university of this final type where I spent my four years,[1] although I am sometimes surprised I ended up there at all. The other kids from my high school honors classes were applying to famous schools with one-word names like Stanford, Tulane, and Duke. I had good grades, but all I really knew was that I wanted to go to Seattle. When you grow up in Eastern Washington, Seattle just seems like the logical next step: that was where all of the cool things were. Living in Spokane was like an internship leading up to residence in Seattle. To start over again in a small town like South Bend or Durham would be a step backward. I was also fairly certain I wanted to go to a Christian university, because, as an impressionable Christian teenager, I had an inkling that I might otherwise be exposed to "the world" too much and maybe "lose my faith," or something worse. These possibilities were vaguely intimated at youth group—sure, you *could* go to a "non-Christian" college, the youth pastor told us, but did you really want to go to a place where they taught evolution and postmodernism, where people were having sex and drinking every weekend?[2] I didn't know what I wanted to do, so my mother made what seemed a saner argument: I could either go to a state school, where I would be the bizarre, backward, conservative Christian kid, or I could go to the Christian school, where I would be the bizarre liberal kid who reads poetry and listens to weird music.

I decided I was leaning toward the Christian school. Just to make sure, though, I participated in a weekend visit to the Christian university while I was still in high school, and frankly, it seemed like a terrible place. I slept for one night in the dorm room of a guy who had frosted blond hair and was into snowboarding. I guess they put

1. I am not going to mention the name of the school, but it should be painfully obvious.

2. Of course, these things all happen at Christian colleges also—we just didn't talk about them as much.

me on the "jock" floor, which was a pretty big mistake if the school was trying to get me to enroll. The most substantive conversation I overheard between my host and his roommate during the weekend was, "Dude, when we were on that ski trip I could just tell you were diggin' on her; she was diggin' on you, man. You were just totally diggin' on each other." A terrifying future of Christian ski trips and diggin' on blonde girls in GAP sweatshirts unfolded before me, so I buried myself in my security blanket, a well-worn copy of *Catcher in the Rye*, and no fewer than three of the dudes who wandered by the room commented, "That's that book crazy people read." I wrote a letter to a friend beginning with the words *I don't think I could ever go to school here*.

I had also recently taken a tour of the not-Christian university I'd been considering. Even though nobody called me dude or said I was crazy, there was something about the campus that felt oppressive and ugly. Everything was gray and brown, constricting and concrete. The Christian school, in contrast, had well-manicured green lawns and flowers and open spaces. Everyone smiled at you and there were no unwashed white people with dreadlocks. On the Christian school tour, I asked the counselor whether there was much in the way of jazz or rock music on campus. She knew nothing about the jazz program, but rock bands, yes, we have some, she said. There was a band on campus, the Lincolns, and they'd been on the radio, she said. This excited me a little—A band! In Seattle! On the radio!—but on balance, the Christian school was starting to seem like an awful place for higher learning and more like a place where the main curriculum was fashion, diggin' on things, and being upper-middle class. That was what I thought for most of the visit. Until I went to the concert.

Of course there was a concert. Because if we have learned anything about Christian culture, it is that concerts are how they get you. They almost did not get me, because the first act was an embarrassingly earnest ska band from Yakima whose name I will not mention other than to say that it was a Star Wars reference, and once you know you are dealing with a Christian Star Wars ska band, you know what kind of bullshit you're getting into. I sat through forty minutes of painfully "fun" music and wondered if the unlimited free breakfast cereal in the cafeteria was the best thing about this place.

Then the second band came on. And they got me.

Why did an indie rock band convince me to attend a Christian university? Much of what makes music compelling is elusive, and to capture it in words on paper is difficult. For example, I now have the task of explaining why a nondescript three-piece emo band moved me, perhaps even changing the course of my life, and I have nothing but adjectives to turn to. Adjectives are weak words—they are nothing without nouns—and I can't seem to find any nouns with which to eff the ineffable.

What did it for me, I guess, is that the second band didn't say anything at all. They were three very plain-looking white guys who were not named after Star Wars. They did not speak to the audience, but their songs said a lot. I could feel truth and honesty and caring somewhere in the too-loud, distorted pop they were playing. They probably weren't thinking this—they were just kids in a band—but I was feeling it. I stopped thinking about the annoying jocks and started feeling how much love, hope, and faith seemed to be entering my body from the amps and drums in front of me. Later, I bought their record, and the lyrics confirmed that I'd been right. Beautiful sentences like "I was so opposed to changing / I was ready to deny / a sense of gratitude for learning / how to love" and "no one's brave enough to stand alone" and "what can I offer you to make me see," the latter strained out desperately, a plea and a prayer. Their music didn't sound like Petra or dc Talk; it sounded like XTC, Blur, or Ride, bands I was only dimly aware of and would later grow to love. People who made music like that came from a university like this. If you want a dramatic conversion narrative: it was this moment, and this band, Wes Dando, that made me decide to attend the Christian school. What can I say? I was just diggin' on 'em.

ENGAGING THE CULTURE, SORT OF

The motto of my university, which was repeated by the school's president a good eight or nine times a day, was "Engaging the culture, changing the world." The second clause is somewhat audacious, though suitably idealistic for any college, but the first part was interesting in the way it suggested that we weren't, in fact, part of "the culture." This is one of the paradoxes of evangelicaldom that I am still just beginning to comprehend: there was "the world," and there was us. There was "the culture," and there was us. The joke, of course, is that we evangelicals were perhaps even more concerned with our own culture-making than "the culture" was. And this culture-that-was-not-culture that we cultivated at the Christian university was indeed a strange laboratory hybrid: one tiny part "the world" to three parts Bible; 100 mL of irreverence to 1,000 mL of reverence; some furtive rebellion, genuine service, dark nights of the soul, and Slurpee (not beer) runs; dashes of intellectual freedom and challenging questions from liberal profs; occasional spontaneous charismatic outbursts of worship music; and occasional spontaneous charismatic outbursts of nude fencing.[3] We "engaged the culture" while remaining inside what we affectionately referred to as "the bubble" of our campus, where *The Princess Bride* was everyone's favorite movie and keggers were strictly root beer affairs.

If you spend any time in a world where people go to this kind of college, you hear rumors of certain ridiculous rules and regulations. Some of them are not true, like the No Dancing Rule. Dancing was never outlawed at my school—there were just no university-sponsored dances. If somebody wanted to host a dance, there was a loophole in the rules that allowed "instructional" dances. I remember being taught the Electric Slide by an actual professional dance instructor during my first year, which, to be honest, was a pretty useful skill to have later in life—certainly more useful than the physics class I was forced to take. The swing craze was on its way out in "the culture," which meant it was just arriving for us, and it became a boon, because it was one of those "instructional" dances where you actually got to touch a member of the opposite sex. The instructional-dancing-only policy was finally repealed the year after I graduated, following decades of protest from students, and perhaps in response to a very successful (and dry) dance party held by some students off-campus, called the Funk-Tion. The Funk-Tion sold hundreds of tickets and featured actual professors tending bar (though the students who organized the event were careful not to supply any alcohol, in order to prove a point to the administration), and everybody had a good time, even if some of us felt guilty afterward for having spent

3. This may have been the most glorious moment in the university's long history.

a good portion of the evening dancing with a girl who was not our girlfriend.[4] Soon after the administrators caved, the first-ever official school dance was cancelled due to low ticket sales.

Aside from the dancing, there was also the infamous Enforced Chapel Rule, which in my first year meant that you had to fill out a Scantron sheet verifying your attendance at various church events. Fortunately, the school implemented the honor system (or the "feel free to lie and say you went to chapel ten times this quarter when you only went twice" system), which worked well for most of us—people who wanted to go to chapel stuff went, and people who didn't want to go lied about it. They also allowed us to count semi-do-gooder activities as legitimate chapel-related events, like being a DJ on the college's radio station or tutoring ESL students.

So some of the stereotypes about the rules weird religious people follow at their colleges are based on a kernel of truth. But some of our peculiarities are not so much iron-fisted authoritarian precepts as they are obnoxious. Such as: wherever two or more students are gathered (for almost any reason), it is a foregone conclusion that one of them will produce an acoustic guitar, and it will be only a matter of minutes before they will start singing a praise & worship song. As of this writing, the photo on the front page of my school's Web site depicts two floppy-haired dudes playing an acoustic guitar and a djembe on the middle of the quad. During my time they would have been playing "Open the Eyes of My Heart," a U2-style ditty with one verse and one chorus, each repeated about seventy thousand times. This song and others like it were performed every Wednesday night at a gathering known as GROUP. Please do not ask me to explain why GROUP is called GROUP. I mean, obviously it's a thinly veiled attempt to keep the spirit of youth group going on into one's early twenties by the clever omission of the word "youth" from the name, but what I can't tell you is why it was called GROUP, in ALL CAPS—as in "You ARE going to GROUP this week, AREN'T you? You DO believe in GOD, right?" A few years ago I called up the Office of Campus Ministries to ask why GROUP was called GROUP, but no one there seemed to know. The best answer I got was that they wanted to make it stand out in the text on fliers and posters, but my impression from

---

4. I mean, hypothetically. Also, it may have hypothetically involved a dance known as "the Fishing Rod," but I wouldn't really know.

the word is one of self-importance: the only other word you see regularly written that way is the LORD in the Bible.

And yes, any Christian college is not short on well-scrubbed, khaki-and-white-shirt-wearing, Jars of Clay-liking,[5] GROUP-going students. Strict rules on sex are in place, banning carnal relations of the premarital, extramarital, and homosexual variety. This didn't stop the students who really wanted to engage in the first, and I can't imagine how the latter two would have been punished had they been discovered. Drinking and smoking are also anathema, even for those of legal age, and it was always cringingly sad to see smart, respectable deans toe the Board of Trustees line, justifying this kind of nonsense. I remember a speech given by one of the deans after quite a few students had vocally opposed the rule; her explanations were so half-hearted it seemed as if she much rather would have said, "Actually, it doesn't matter whether or not you have a cold one on a Friday night. We all have more important things to worry about." But she couldn't. She was trapped by the traditions of our school's particular religious denomination, even though the most common church background at my school was "nondenominational."[6] And in a way, so were we, although as long as you didn't get on a soapbox about booze and cigarettes, or any other vice, it was easy enough to indulge: just don't do it in the dorm or buy it at the 7-11 across the street from campus, and you'll probably get away with it.

This all makes Christian college sound like a hotbed of spirit-crushing oppression, but the surprising part is that it didn't feel like that at all. I enjoyed almost every minute of it. The people who really felt oppressed by the atmosphere had a simple solution: they brazenly, repeatedly violated rules they knew they would be expelled for breaking, and most were happy to leave. Those who stuck around, like me, found out that beneath the veneer of sanctimony and peer pressure to sing worship songs, there was a beautiful world of life-changing ideas. My best friends and biggest dreams came to me during my four years there. And the biggest secret of all, I found, is that my so-called stiflingly conservative Christian college was one of the best places to make rock music I have ever known.

5. I actually do still like Jars of Clay, to be fair.
6. This does not mean *nonreligious*. It means *really religious, but not Baptist*.

Hear me out. Here's a close-knit community of liberal arts students who already possess basic songwriting skills, having learned to play guitar at Bible camp. Add to that professors who are into super-hip music—there were a number of Nick Cave fanatics, and in one memorable class, my English prof defended Eminem to a classroom of incredulous goody-goodies.[7] We had access to an expensive sound system (ask a sound guy; Christians always have the priciest high-end gear), and anyone with legitimate ties to a campus organization could rent it on the cheap. Then take into account that some of Seattle's best independent record stores are within walking distance of the university bubble. Consider the evangelical fervor for starting clubs that have officers and mission statements and T-shirts with mindless slogans like "UNITY AMIDST DIVERSITY SERVANT LEADERSHIP RETREAT 1999," which can later be worn in an ironic fashion. There are the mildly subversive, arts-friendly organizations like the radio station (more about that later) and the annual music and arts journal, the only place students can (and do!) use the F-word with impunity. Most crucially, almost everyone, regardless of major or denomination, is heavily invested in culture-making. We are the people who brought you the Reformation, abolitionism, and Psalty the singing Bible, after all. There was no reason for our school not to be a haven of rock & roll creativity.

Many local, and even national, bands that went on to make a name for themselves in the greater indie rock world consist at least partly of graduates from my humble, holy alma mater. A spate of bands whose names would surely be familiar to indie hipsters in Seattle and even cross-country, like Fair, Acceptance, Anberlin, Josh Ottum, the Catch, James Pants, Barcelona, and In Praise of Folly, all got their start in part at our humble college. The insular nature of the college, in fact, acted as a hothouse for rock fandom, allowing whichever campus band is most prolific to gain instant mini-fame, to be *the* campus band of the moment. *The band* is like the school's culture-engaging, rocking-out mascot. It's a group of students who play shows both on and off campus, at churches and/or rock clubs and/or bars. All students are aware of *the band*, a number have bought their records, and some have at least one water bottle bearing the band's

---

7. I am 1,000 percent implicating myself in this sentence and any other that appears to cast aspersions on Christian college students.

sticker. Previous *the bands* included the above-mentioned Wes Dando, the above-mentioned Lincolns (who went on to become Wonderful and then United State of Electronica, both mentioned elsewhere in this book), and Trueb (which became a brilliant, short-lived Portland pop band, the Carolines). Even my band was *the band* for a while, which was something of a dream come true for me. Playing our vaguely Christian music in clubs and bars was the kind of thing the university president would have really gotten behind—we were totally engaging the culture.

But while the school's motto was (remember?) "Engaging the culture, changing the world," this was not quite a two-way street; "the culture" was not engaging *us*. As Christians, we felt we had a lot to offer "the world": we were not part of them, but we could impact them in positive ways, with the stuff we got from Jesus. What we lacked was a sense that the culture or the world was going to impact us in any way. We were perfectly happy to, with an almost gnostic superiority, meet the world with our special, secret knowledge and use it to spread special, secret Christian goodness. We were like covert Christian Love Terrorists. Our acts of kindness were in no way random. But the culture, unfortunately, was nowhere to be seen; the people on whom we'd drop our God-bombs did not coexist with us inside the bubble. The only people on campus who were not Christians were the cafeteria workers,[8] and we didn't do a whole lot of "engaging" with them other than asking for more chicken on our Caesar salads.

Being in a band helped a little, but while we were bringing the meaningful artsy stuff to the culture, nobody was bringing the meaningful artsy stuff to the bubble.

I decided to do something about it.

TAKE BACK THE RADIO

According to my own personal mythology, I single-handedly built the campus radio station, and it was a rousing success that forever destroyed the long-lasting American Protestant sacred/secular culture divide, and we put on a ton of great concerts and played great music,

8. This is not entirely true: I met exactly one Muslim and one atheist during my four years there.

and everyone loved me for introducing them to a whole new part of the culture they had never known before.

This is not really what happened. What really happened is that some other people started a radio station, and I took it over and ran it into the ground.

Seizing control of organizations and running them into the ground was something of a hobby for me. My first attempt was sophomore year, when I suddenly became president of a "social justice" club started by five women who were passionately committed to justice and who went on to do incredible kingdom-of-God-type things, and whom I still lovingly refer to as "the Matriarchs," even though I am sure they have forgotten me. The Matriarchs all graduated at the same time, leaving me to run the club, and suddenly, instead of five zealous, mature women leading the group, there was one zealous, immature kid with unkempt facial hair and a few other people who had accompanied our friends to the 1999 WTO protests and who laughed derisively whenever anybody said something that sounded conservative. After months of meetings during which our main accomplishment was agreeing that social awareness is good, we eventually put on an event that had to do with Native American rights, which was meaningful for at least one person that I know of. We also mounted an unsuccessful protest petitioning the university not to solicit students with credit card advertisements. The club was disbanded at the end of the school year.

The problem with college is that you have a whole lot of passion and energy and time, but you do not actually know how to do anything. I know this because I have spent a lot of time on college campuses since my undergraduate days, and it is still happening. When you're twenty years old, earnestness outstrips know-how every time. You try to start or manage important organizations and they don't work out because all you have is ideas, passion, and energy, which may appear to be assets, but which usually just get you into trouble.

Take the radio station, for example. By the time I took control of the station, my senior year, things seemed to be going pretty well. The university had given us $10,000 to start the station a few years back, and we'd finally figured out how to broadcast over the Internet and campus cable TV. A big tech company donated software, we bought all the right licenses to play songs, and because the communications department had no personnel or resources to support us, we found a faculty advisor from the PE department.

This is where the problem started. I said and did a number of stupid things during the course of that year, but the stupidest one was probably deciding to take an adversarial stance toward the only faculty member at the university who was actually offering us help— because he was a PE professor.[9]

Our goals for the fledgling station were mainly to get a lot of free CDs, play them, and put on a few concerts, goals that were moving along at a nice pace: I'd spent the previous year tactlessly e-mailing record companies ("Dear Matador Records, We're starting a radio station, will you please send us your entire back catalog? Thanks!"), so the albums and phone calls from publicists were rolling in regularly. We had enough friends in bands that we could put on stuff like LollapaBumberStock[10] and a Battle of the Bands, and we got a local Domino's to donate one hundred pizzas for various promotional events.[11] Sure, the overarching goal of getting our radio station actually *on the radio*, which would still require a lot of money and legal resources, hadn't come noticeably closer to fruition yet, but that would eventually take care of itself, we assumed.

But when I heard that our advisor was on the board of directors of a Christian radio station and that he had an idea for us to spend one evening a week at the station—let's call it KGOD—producing a conservative Christian talk show, my red pop-culture blood turned cold. If there was one thing we did not want our radio station to be, it was another drop in the Christian subculture ocean. This was our chance to create a tangible artifact of culture-making that was truly bidirectional—not only would we be engaging the culture, we'd be bringing the culture to us and our peers—and the scary alternative facing us looked like the fast track to becoming a Focus on the Family affiliate.

9. This may have to do with my memories of high school and junior high PE, which can be boiled down to the sentence, "Hartse, you run like a queer!"

10. A concert named after the music festivals Lollapalooza, Bumbershoot, and Woodstock. *We* thought it was cool.

11. I sometimes think that my self-worth can best be measured in the number of pizzas I am able to obtain at one time.

My first meeting with the advisor didn't make much sense. I wanted to talk about music and concerts, and in response he told me about the things he heard coming from the PA system in the weight room.[12] He told me that the athletes like to listen to rap songs about "rear entry sex," which, he said, he didn't think would make the alumni of our Christian college very happy. I had to agree: a middle-aged graduate of a Christian college probably would not want to hear a rap song about "rear entry sex." Neither did I, particularly, but why were we even talking about this? And why did he keep using the phrase "rear entry sex" when we'd only met two minutes ago? This, I thought, was a warning sign. And so, when the idea to produce the Christian talk show came up, the staff decided to take a stand.

I spent a week painstakingly composing a letter to our advisor about why we didn't want to do the show, going out of my way to be complimentary to everyone involved, explaining that while we would love to pursue some kind of relationship with KGOD, working on a Christian talk show was not quite the vision we had in mind. I heard nothing back from him until he resigned as our advisor the week before school started, leaving us locked out of our station as per the school's law about student clubs: no advisor, no club. I ran into our music director, Jon, the morning I got the e-mail back from the advisor. I greeted him in the spirit of brotherly, Christian, culture-engaging love.

"Jon," I said, "We're fucked."

INDIER THAN THOU

Desperate phone calls and e-mails flew, and within a week the advisor agreed to come back on a provisional basis. Our radio station was saved, and we lived another day to host rock shows and pudding-wrestling contests. I wished things had gone better with the advisor, but I was mostly just happy that the radio station was going to continue, because I knew how much I had needed and wanted something like it when I started college, and I knew that there would be a new group of students coming in who would stay at the school

12. I did not know our university had a weight room, but I knew the best place to get soy chai lattes.

specifically, and maybe only, because of the community they found at the station. The transition to college can be a spiritually volatile time, when kids are forced to really consider their entire identities for the first time, and if they were anything like me, the new freshmen were in for a tectonic change.

When I first arrived in my dorm room, I put up a poster of the Christian punk band MxPx, but quickly learned that even at a Christian college this was slightly uncool, especially when compared to the Radiohead posters and Japanese pin-up girls on the wall of my across-the-hall neighbor. It was time to draw on my last few years of reading *CMJ* and really immerse myself in what used to be called "college music" and was now called "indie rock." Within a matter of months, I had dozens of new favorite bands. I ditched Jars of Clay for Death Cab for Cutie, and I quickly got indier-than-thou. Tooth & Nail was out; Barsuk, Matador, Sub Pop, Merge, Touch and Go, 4AD, and Saddle Creek were in. I knew that there was nothing more authentic than indie rock. I knew that any band on a major label was stupid. I also had a LiveJournal blog, the entries of which were often titled with indie rock lyrics. I wore horn-rimmed glasses and vintage puffy vests.

This was like a bizarre inversion of my early teenage years. I used to pretend that listening to Christian rock made me cool because it was indie, but during my years at the radio station, I started to believe that listening to indie rock made me righteous, because indie was more in line with godly values. To the indie evangelist, indie rock is not only a genre, it's a way of life. It means seeking out and participating in communities that form around music, not around profit or political agendas. It means thinking seriously about the music we purchase and from whom we're buying it. When I buy a record, who is getting my money? Is this a fake Christian indie owned by a multinational corporation that is marketed to look like it's an independent artsy label?[13] It means, perhaps, valuing artists who write their own songs, produce their own records, and are given the freedom to write about what they care about and are not paid to name-drop Jesus. It probably means not buying cash-in greatest hits collections and not listening to Christian radio monopolies.

13. You should know, for example, that EMI owns 49 percent of Tooth & Nail Records.

I can still get behind most of that, and I sincerely believed it for a few years, but I no longer have the energy to *preach it* like I used to. Indie was part of our mission statement at the radio station: we somehow found a way to connect the values of the music we were playing, the importance of creativity and artistry and spirituality and relationships, to a verse from Ecclesiastes. The exhausting part of being a Christian and an indie rock fan—a baptized snob—is that it is hard to know which Man to stand up to. There's the regular old corporate Man, the one everybody who is not necessarily Christian always wants to stick it to, and he still needs to have it stuck to. Then there is the Christian Establishment, the one that tells you to listen to KGOD and read books by Joel Osteen and put a Jesus-fish-eating-Darwin-fish emblem on your car, and you know that's not what it's all about, so you have to stick it to that Man. *Then* you have to stick it to the Man who tells you that *your* sticking is misguided because you are a Christian and that you are on the wrong side, the side of the bigots and the evil businessmen and the liars, because you know you are not on that side. You also have to stick it to anybody who is sticking it to the Man in the wrong way—with a malicious spirit of mockery and hatred instead of your spirit of Christ-minded revolution and transformation.

What I'm saying is that you are going to have to do a lot of sticking it to somebody.[14] It gets tiring. I don't recommend it, even though I still recommend the music. The truth is, indie as a philosophy doesn't have much to do with indie rock as a genre, and both have surely been twisted and appropriated since they began. If Modest Mouse, Built to Spill, and Sonic Youth, three well-known bands who record for major labels, can all be called "indie rock," there isn't anything particularly indie about it. But what indie rock and Christian rock have in common, and what I've learned as a fan (at times) of both, is how important belief and identity is for any music scene, and for any community, in fact. In both cases, there is rarely one unifying factor that can be said to make a genre what it is—the lyrics, the sound, whatever—except for the idea that *we're all in this together*. The very idea of a *fan* (short for *fanatic*) offers a clue about what drives any scene in the pop world: people's personal and social investment in it, or even, dare I say, their love.

14. Yes, I realize this sounds dirty.

As Captain and Tennille told us, love will keep us together. And as Joy Division also told us, love will tear us apart. It kept together a small cadre of indie-minded Christian college students who believed in music, and it also threatened to tear our radio station apart. I might have been a little pig-headed with the PE professor, but you have to believe me when I say I did it out of love.

FIVE ALBUMS THAT MADE ME FEEL HIP IN COLLEGE

Wes Dando, *The Tired Hours* (Fracaso, 2001)

There's a danger in continuing to mention obscure, out-of-print records by bands that only made one thousand copies of their records, but if you look hard enough (I have seen this one in used bins in more than one country, even!), you can find this CD by the band who tricked me into going to a Christian college. It looks like an unremarkable eight-song EP, but the poetic cadences of Erick Newbill's cutting, honest voice, the inverted bass lines, and the climactic two-song album closers "Throughout the Earth" and "As Bravery Crumbles" make this record a lot more special than most other college basement projects. *The Tired Hours* was produced by Aaron Sprinkle before he started producing every Christian rock record in sight, and because it came out before the advent of the "loudness wars" that make every album released today sound like a busy freeway,[15] the click and buzz of the instruments feels warm and organic. I liked this record so much that I convinced my friends to pay Erick several hundred dollars to record our first demo of awful songs

United State of Electronica, *United State of Electronica* (Sonic Boom, 2004)

U.S.E. is not an electronica act in the traditional sense of the word: they have a live drummer, electric guitars, and a bassist. They're really a rock band with a constantly thudding four-on-the-floor bass-drum beat coming from someplace, a synthesizer, and a vocoder.[16] And what they do is, they play super-optimistic

15. "SCCHHHHHHHHHHHHHHHHHHHHHHHHHHHHHHHHHSSSAAAAAAHHSSC CCHHHHHHHHHHHHHHHHHHH"

16. A vocoder, to get all technical on you, is a device that allows a user to modulate the pitch and timbre of one sound (usually the human voice) with

high-energy dance music for the Lord. They don't *mention* the Lord, but if you listen carefully, you'll find on this record (and anything else they have done since) a relentless celebration of such heady theological topics as love, dancing, fun, beach parties, music, and love. It's the love that really makes all the difference between U.S.E. and somebody like Andrew W.K.[17] U.S.E. is nothing short of evangelistic—Every. Single. Song. Is about Love—and I'll be damned if they're not engaging the culture and changing the world. You win, Christian college.

Death Cab for Cutie, *Transatlanticism* (Barsuk, 2003)

The band's third and best record, in my opinion, transcends their earlier set pieces on lost love. Although "We Looked Like Giants" is a juggernaut of a track about university romance, it's the grand thesis statement of its title track that moves this record from the earthly to the heavenly. "Transatlanticism" builds and builds (and builds and builds and builds), driven by drummer Jason McGerr's feral pounding on the mantra "I need you so much closer," which is probably about a lover but speaks to a human desire to really know the things we love. It works as a cry to a God who chooses not to show himself too, obviously, as both a plea and a demand, morphing by the song's end into a tender but earnest prayer.

Iron & Wine, *Our Endless Numbered Days* (Sub Pop, 2004)

Albums like *Our Endless Numbered Days* are what I'm fairly confident I'll still be listening to in twenty or thirty years. The timeless quality certainly comes from the instrumentation and melodies (but for the crisp production, this could have been recorded in 1930), but Sam Beam's strength comes from his ability to write intimate lyrics that appeal to universal truths. There's a tragic resilience about the characters in Beam's songs, who are acutely aware

---

another sound (like a synthesizer or guitar) electronically. In other words, it's a magic box that makes your voice sound like a robot. A vocoder is the reason you hate Cher's "Life after Love" and love Daft Punk's "Harder Better Faster Stronger."

17. I do recommend listening to Andrew W. K., although I can't say there is a whole lot of meaty spiritual/intellectual stuff to wrap your brain around on tracks like "Party Hard" and "Party til You Puke." But he smashed himself in the face with a brick for the photo shoot for his debut album, and that counts for something.

of their mortality. "Naked as We Came" is especially powerful. It makes me think of a night my wife and I had this record on, before we were married, and we were laying on my couch and looking up at the ceiling and wondering what we'd do tomorrow and the next day and so on, and even though this song is about lovers who know that one of them is going to have to bury the other, it made me feel like I knew what was around the bend and that it was going to be worthwhile. Beam knows this, and I know this, just like I know I'll fight with Sarah, and we'll make up, and we'll have more great days and more fights and so on until we die, that our love, and all love, is the reason we are here, and whatever's coming will be sweet and sad and beautiful. Like this record.

 Bis, *Social Dancing* (Wiiija, 1999)

I have only met one other person in my whole life who likes Bis. It was a guy who looked exactly like me and later took over my job at the campus radio station. Bis is a Scottish trio who called themselves Manda Rin, John Disco, and Sci-Fi Steven and were a bizarre and clashing pastiche of riot grrrl, punk, techno, disco, ska, Nintendo, queer politics, anime, skater culture, dance music, and pop. This should not work. But Bis's albums are so full of energy and power that I cannot stop myself from loving even ridiculous songs like "I'm a Slut" and "Shopaholic," both of which appear on *Social Dancing*. More mature songs like "Theme from Tokyo" and "Detour" bridge a divide between the band's earlier sugary dance rock (the single "Kandy Pop" is the best and worst kind of earworm, relentless in both annoyance and catchiness) and their later contemplative trip-hop. I didn't even mention Bis in this chapter; I just love them.

9

I Could Sing of Your Love for Ten or Fifteen Minutes

WORSE HIP MUSIC

One of the things you hear Christians talk about a lot is "worship." In theory, worship, in its original meaning, as in *to give worth and honor to God*, is what we do all the time, regardless of the activity we happen to be doing. In practice, though, when somebody says, "Now let's worship," what they mean is, "Now I will play the guitar, and we will sing repetitive pop songs about God for about thirty minutes."

As far as I know, worship music as it existed when I was singing it in church as a kid and as it exists now is based on the following principles:

1. God is good.
2. Singing songs is good.
3. Therefore, singing songs about God is good.
4. There are a lot of songs that people have written about God that we could sing.
5. However, we should not sing "traditional" church music or hymns in church because either:
    a. young people don't like it, so they will quit going to church and then listen to Elton John or Slayer instead; or

b. hymns are not relevant to people today because of lyrics like "Here I raise mine Ebeneezer"[1] and/or because of four-part harmony, which we do not understand how to do without a lot of training.

There might be other, better explanations you could come up with as far as evangelical church music is concerned; I could probably whip something up about God-inspired, innovative artistry and cultural relevance and throw in a Bible quote about singing a "new song" if you gave me a few minutes. But as far as I'm concerned, points one through four are relatively uncontroversial and reasonable in almost any church, evangelical or otherwise, whereas the fifth point is uniquely evangelical. And, frankly, it is pretty ridiculous.

I think I believed it was ridiculous even when I was a kid, despite the fact that I liked the songs we were singing. We sang dumbed-down songs, like "I Believe in Jesus," which is kind of a kindergarten version of the creeds set to the clunkiest chord arrangement this side of the Steve Miller Band's "The Joker." I usually didn't sing during church, mostly because I was embarrassed about how loud my dad was singing and I didn't want to draw more attention to myself than was necessary, but also because everything we were singing just felt clumsily obvious. There are only so many ways to communicate "God is good" with three chords, and Christians can run out of ideas rather quickly. My favorite church services were always the Christmas ones, the ones where we sang actual traditional hymn-like songs, the kind that people had actually been singing for hundreds of years, instead of the kinds that had been sung since 1980, which had all the histori-cal and spiritual significance of a Michael Bolton ballad.

Until I was about fourteen, the entirety of my exposure to Christian music was through church and Christian radio. I was vaguely aware of hymns, though I was not sure what made them different from "worship songs," so I wasn't prepared for what went on during the Catholic services I started attending in high school. There weren't many such services—we only had a required all-school Mass a few times a year, and there was the tragic funeral of my class-mate Justin, who had been joking around with us at lunch the week

1. Which, granted, is a totally weird thing to hear a congregation of three hundred people sing.

before—but the ones I attended had gravitas. It sounds funny to say, but until then I did not realize that centuries-old ritual and tradition could play a part in worship.

While I was having this revelation, the Catholics were trying to get hip to the jive the evangelicals were plying. I remember a particularly valiant attempt to contemporarify one of the unpopular required Masses, one of the ones held in the gym.[2] The priests had recruited one of the kids who played in the percussion section with me in second-period band. They had him playing drums during a terminally unrockable sung section of the liturgy: "Christ has died, Christ is risen, Christ will come again," and then a few minutes later to the same tune, "a-amen, a-amen, a-a-a-amen." He filled his post admirably, gently padding at the drums, using brushes (sticks would have been a bit much), with no emotion whatsoever. He stared stoically ahead, which is exactly the right attitude for a drummer who has been forced to play music that doesn't need or want drums.

I knew the music played at my church was cheesy, but unlike that Mass, at least the drums were *necessary* for the upbeat pop songs we were playing. It may be that low-church Protestants are conscious of a certain lack of reverence in our swapping of liturgy for the music + sermon model, and perhaps we attempt to recover this gravity through the chunky power chords, throbbing bass, and pounding drums[3] of our worship music. "If you've never been ministered to by a bass line before, get ready," I remember a youth pastor saying during a worship gathering once. An absurd statement, but perhaps it is because we had never been ministered to by four-part choral harmonies in church that we were open to hearing what four thick, roundwound strings had to say about the Holy Spirit.

---

2. The other thing I remember about these services is that whenever the priest prayed for anybody using the "laying on of hands" method, everybody in the gym was encouraged to stretch their hands toward that person, as if we were touching them, the result of which was one thousand Catholic high school students performing the Nazi salute.

3. Regrettably, some churches use electronic drums so they can have complete control over the sound mix. This is morally wrong and sinful.

BEING MISERABLE BUILDS CHARACTER

I do sometimes wish that evangelicals—that I—could be less desirous of rocking and more modest about the instrumental accompaniment to our songs of praise. I myself am guilty of hamming it up on stage[4] from time to time, so I thank God that during the two years I was playing drums at my church in Seattle, I was strategically hidden behind a screen upon which the song lyrics were projected. I also played in rock bands in Seattle, and my approach to playing music in the two settings was essentially the same: it was something like, *Hey, I'm enjoying this!* I didn't mean it to come across as showy; I just like to rock out with my enthusiasm out.[5]

I had nowhere to hide, however, at the church we went to in a small town in northern California while I was in grad school. I was playing bass, and given that church-song bass lines are mind-bogglingly simple,[6] you have to find ways to make it interesting. My way was to pretend I was Evan Cranley, a creative bassist who plays in the Montreal-based bands Stars and Broken Social Scene. I made up melody-driven bass lines that go way up high on the tiny strings, and then I moved around a little while playing—not a *lot*, but enough to get ambivalent comments from congregants about my playing. One woman, after watching me play, complimented me on my "heart," which I didn't understand but found meaningful and moving.[7] Another woman mentioned that after church, her son jumped around and acted like he was playing some kind of crazy guitar, pretending to be me.

Maybe I became an enthusiastic worship music guy, but my actual opinions about rock & roll in church are mixed. I like rock music and I like going to church, and they both mean a lot to me, but I am not totally sure I want to do them at the same time. They are both easy to do badly, in a shoddy, showy, ugly way, and when you get the two done that way together, the effect is almost unbearable.

4. Yes, we have a *stage* in evangelical churches.

5. That's the last time I do that, I promise.

6. Actual transcript of the chords to one popular song we played: "A B (repeat x 10)."

7. She might have meant it in the *Captain Planet* sense.

Rock & roll, or at least bad, three-chords-and-a-clunky-lyric rock & roll, doesn't stand up under the weight of the earth-shaking good news we mean to proclaim. That's not to say that gospel and guitars can never work together—of course they can, and rockers have every right to sing about Jesus, just like God has every right to move mysteriously in people's hearts through a shitty Evanescence song. But the songs we play and the way we play them ought to be good. Surely this is not an unreasonable request; the songs ought to be interesting and moving and full of life. Whether they are praises or laments, they ought to communicate the human-God relationship in a nuanced and textured and lovely way. And so much rock music that is played in churches simply is *not* that, which makes me kind of hate it.

I hate standing in church and singing "Open the Eyes of My Heart" a hundred times in a row until I don't know what we're talking about anymore. The most depressing thing I have ever heard is the part of "I Could Sing of Your Love Forever" that talks about how "the world" doesn't understand why Christians love God so much but that when they get to know him, they will get it, and they will "dance with joy like we're dancing now." I have heard that there are churches where people dance, and I'm sure they have a good time with that song, but I personally have never witnessed anything *close* to dancing during that song, which is pretty much a mid-tempo shuffle that just *plods* along. To dance to it would be the most awkward and unnatural thing possible. The closest we got to physical outbursts of joy at my church was clapping on beats one and three. If we were honest, we would have sung about how, instead of dancing, we were "awkwardly swaying and halfheartedly clapping with joy while singing quietly so nobody else can hear us." The miles-wide chasm between that song's lyrics and reality is such that I think most churches have given up playing it.

I also squirm when I sing lyrics I'm not sure I believe, something like "Lord, you're all I want," because to be honest I want a whole lot of other things more than I want the Lord, like lunch and to be out of debt. I roll my eyes when worship leaders try to get people to clap, or they say, "Come on, church," or they start improvising new lyrics and melodies over the chorus so that the congregation gets confused about whether they are supposed to follow the worship leader or keep singing the real song. I cannot bear songs that repeat their one and only verse seven or eight or twelve times. I cringe at the sheer audacity and self-centeredness of songs that are allegedly about God; for example, I once heard a worship song lyric—I wish I were making this up—that says to God, "You journal about me every day."

A secret, though: as much as I hate this music, I love playing it. I remember a *Calvin and Hobbes* strip where Calvin puts on his father's glasses and imitates him: "Calvin, go do something you hate! Being miserable builds character!" Turns out he's right. I get into a weird Zen-like state where I have space to move around in the songs— nobody's really paying attention to what I'm doing, because they are (probably) having their own meaningful worship experience with the Lord, so I do a lot of noodly stuff up high on the neck, try to come up with new ways to voice the same old chords, and learn things about myself and my instrument and the way songs work. If I'm playing the drums, I add strange fills and then try to wait until halfway through the next measure to end them. I give myself weird limitations, like to play on as few drums as possible or to hit the snare drum as little as possible in a given song, or I try to figure out how my favorite drummers do what they do. I don't know if my fellow churchgoers have ever noticed just how much Mates of State or Appleseed Cast I listen to, but it's there in my playing. Above all, I don't forget that I am *playing* the drums, and I think this playing makes me a more creative and sensitive and attentive person, somehow.

Playing songs I hate has made me realize that what I do when I play worship songs is a service to my community, and therefore, a service to God. If my drumming can be a small part of what helps to usher people into the presence of God, I am all for it. Sometimes I even feel the presence of God myself, though I am rarely sure that's what it is. I don't remember what the still small voice said to Elijah, but usually it says to me, "This is awesome and we are totally rocking out!" If that's God, I'll take it.

GIVE UP

I first started playing worship music in the youth group at the mega- church my family attended. I learned how to play the guitar (and the drums to some extent) there, and the adults and fellow teenagers who led the worship team were sincere and kind, but music was a big, sacred deal, and mysterious things were always happening with the other members of the "worship team." People were frequently asked to stop playing with us because they had to "get right with God." A couple of guys would frequently get put on probation because they'd confessed to the youth pastor that they smoked pot recently. (As I recall, this only warranted something like a three-week suspension.) Some people even got called on the carpet by the leaders because of hunches that they weren't "serious" about their faith, to which they'd always confess, and then, after some serious soul-searching, they would come back to the team.

I was never asked to do this, which is either because I was a good kid or because I avoided everything about youth group except for playing music, and so the youth pastors really had no idea who I was. There was one thing, though, that scared me about the way we treated music at my youth group: there was this persistent idea that if you *really* loved music, God might ask you—force you—to give it up. Jason, an adopted Korean kid, was our prime example. Despite being raised by a white family, he managed to fall comfortably into the classic stereotypical Asian Piano Prodigy role, practicing for hours on end each day. God gave Jason his talent for playing the piano, our youth pastor told us, after Jason had played a jaw-dropping, blazingly fast rendition of a classical piece. But God might ask Jason to give up the piano one day, the pastor continued. Would Jason give up the piano for God? Yes, he would, he told us. And if God asked you to give up something *you* love, something *you* have devoted your life to, what would you do?

Another kid, also a musician, piped up, and said that God had recently demanded something of him. "He said, 'Mark, give me the blues.' So now when I play the B-flat blues, it's for God."

Immediately, I thought of my PFR wall, thirty square feet of my bedroom that was covered in photos, articles, stickers, autographed posters, and other memorabilia dedicated to my favorite Christian band. I was terrified, and I knew suddenly that God was going to ask me to give up PFR. I was scared and upset. *Wait a minute, God,* I said. *This hardly seems fair. PFR is a Christian band! Their songs are all about you! I love them because they write these great songs and have awesome guitar solos, but all the words are about you! And wasn't it you who made me love music in the first place?*

After a few days of going back and forth like this, I decided that God wasn't asking me to give up PFR, or music, or anything I liked. God made me, and it seemed reasonable that he made me to like stuff. That's what I didn't get—why was there this insistence that God regularly asks us to give up things we love, things we in essence were created to do, "for him"? What was he going to have us do instead? Stuff we didn't like? If so, he reminded me of Calvin's dad. If God wanted me to give up the thing I loved, to stop listening to PFR or stop playing the drums or stop listening to the radio, he was just being unreasonable, because I felt more excited when the bass player started jamming on the Cranberries' "Zombie" during worship practice than I did when we were slogging through another verse of "Awesome God."[8]

I kept thinking about what Mark had said, too, and it didn't add up. *That* is what God demands of you when you have to pick up your cross and carry it? That stuff about the poor and loving your enemies and the fatherless and the widow, that stuff is all totally good, but what God really wanted was for Mark to think about him while playing the blues in a particular key on alto saxophone? That sounded bogus to me, but I could appreciate Mark's devotion. Perhaps I should "give God" my love of music, I thought. Then again, I saw no reason to stop there; I figured I should give everything to God, including music. Wasn't that, truly, what we meant when we talked about worship?

God never asked me to "give up" music, as far as I know, so I am still at it whenever possible. I play in bands when I can, and if I can't, I listen to it constantly. I haven't "given" music to God, but I don't think I have any authority whatsoever to do so anyway.[9] To me, the act of playing worship music is a surrender to God. I lay down my prejudices, something that is generally impossible for me to do as a

8. I have nothing but respect and admiration for Rich Mullins. He was a genius and full of compassion and grace and love, moreso than probably anyone else who has been associated with CCM. But *man*, "Awesome God" is not his finest hour.

9. My favorite band, Sixpence None the Richer, is named for a C. S. Lewis passage about humans being unable to give God any gifts, since everything in the world is already his.

music critic and general know-it-all jerk, and I play simple plunkety-plunk songs that under normal circumstances would not move me any more than a Danielle Steele novel or a Matchbox 20 album.[10] And two incredible things happen. One is that because of something I do, people feel—no, I'll dare to say they *are*—closer to God. Not because I am a great drummer or bass player, but because I show up to do what I know how to do. The second thing that happens is that somehow, even when I don't believe the words everyone else is singing, I get closer to God, too. It's kind of a miracle.

Before I started playing music myself, I used to watch the people on stage, the worship team, at church. They seemed so professional, so *into* what they were doing: the worship leader, with his designer glasses and Northwest-casual sweater, closed his eyes, tilting his head skyward. The backup singers did modest dances in place and started the claps by gently rapping one palm on the wrist of the hand holding the microphone. The bass player bobbed his head to the groove the way all bass players do. The drummer, a kid just a few years older than I was, rocked out with nervous energy.

But there was one guy, the electric guitarist, who didn't bob or weave or close his eyes. He was a slight, pale man with a mullet, wearing a faded sweatshirt and a pencil-thin child-molester moustache, and he was the only one on stage who did not confidently project a middle-class suburban confidence. In his hands was a red Gibson SG, which he rarely looked up from, never smiling, always focused on the music and his own modest ornamentations—a few riffs, and once in a while, a solo. *What's that guy's problem,* I used to think.

Dorothy Sayers wrote that "the only Christian work is good work, done well," and evangelicals have gotten so lost in the hand-wringing about how to present an authentic simulation of secular rock music so that people (who, exactly?) will take us seriously that we have forgotten what it means to just play well. When I see a worship leader with carefully mussed hair trying too hard to be breathily, sensually worshipful, I think back to the guitarist in the sweatshirt. I used to think he was doing it wrong, but now I know he was focusing on the only thing that made any sense to him: playing music the best he could, for himself, his people, and the Lord.

10. Perhaps I am being unfair to Danielle Steele here.

FIVE ALBUMS THAT ARE NOT REALLY WORSHIP MUSIC AT ALL, IN A GOOD WAY

 Rich Mullins, *A Liturgy, a Legacy, and a Ragamuffin Band* (Reunion, 1993)

To be honest, I don't think I have ever actually owned a "worship album," unless you count a couple of things I illegally download-ed just to see what they sounded like. I've heard (and probably played) my share of Matt Redman songs in churches, but the only mainstream worship-song dude I have ever really liked was Rich Mullins. This record begins "allow me to make this disclaimer, everybody: I'm barely ready to do this, but let's keep doing it." I can't think of a better way to start an album about trying to understand God's love and what to do about it. Mullins is always eloquent and honest, and his hardcore belief songs (like "Creed," a musical version of the Apostles' Creed) fit comfortably along-side his blunt *I don't get it* songs (like "Hard" and "I'll Carry On"). Anybody who can write a song called "We Are Not as Strong as We Think We Are" is somebody you want on your side when life isn't making sense.

 Urban Hymnal, *Don't Go Hiding* (self-released, 2008)

I have a handful of worship records made by people I know (some friends from Church of the Apostles in Seattle made one several years ago called *Ordo*, which I love), but the sheer scope and ambi-tion of Urban Hymnal, a project my friend Zadok[11] put together with some other musicians from the large middle-section of a Venn diagram where the Seattle indie rock scene and the Seattle Christian community meet. Their songs are epic, soaring, and emotional, full of post-rock pomp and circumstance. "Love Is Fear," from this album, is a quintessential Urban Hymnal track in the way it manages to convey both worship and frustration at once, and in the way it blends rock with liturgical solemnity. I often daydream, when I listen to my favorite music, that I am actually the drummer in the band, and sometimes it takes me hours or days to snap out of the fantasy that I will be at a Death Cab for Cutie show, during which Jason McGerr will break both his arms, and someone will shout, "Quick! Is there anybody here who can play Death Cab's

---

11. I don't really think it's necessary for me to mention his last name. If you know a Zadok, I am pretty sure we are talking about the same guy.

entire catalog on the drums?" I also sometimes have this fantasy about Urban Hymnal; I imagine the joy of being the one to make all that lovely, reverb-drenched noise, to make those drums and cymbals ring out in a cathedral a million miles long.

Stars, *Heart* (Arts & Crafts, 2003)

Maybe I don't actually believe you can be "ministered to" by a bass line—not really—but I can say that Evan Cranley's bass playing on *Heart*, the second and loveliest[12] album by Stars, is almost sacramental. It is something solid and tangible on a record that tends, occasionally, toward the airy-fairy or at least the hippy-dippy. Guitars and keyboards twinkle, and the love songs (they are all love songs) are heavenly, but it is those gently assertive bass lines that anchor the tunes, that give them weight and body. So few rock bass players can effectively play in the upper register without being distracting, but Cranley knows the subtle alchemy between rhythm and melody. I cannot help being moved to a higher[13] plane when I hear the hidden track, "The Comeback," and while I will resist making the conceptual leap that would baptize the song as a crypto-Christian commentary on Jesus's return, I cannot help feeling all the joy and possibility in the world even as Torquil Campbell sings a celebration of drugs, sex, and booze.[14]

PFR, *Great Lengths* (Vireo, 1994)

PFR were a musically conservative rock band, and this is the secret that made them better than almost any of their big-name Christian rock peers; they were not trying to be cool, they were just trying to sound like the Beatles. I have never been so excited about the release of an album as I was on January 10, 1995, when this record was released. PFR had been my all-time favorite band for over a year, and I was in the absolute throes of first pop love—the band could do no wrong, and every note, from the fake strings on "Great Lengths" to Patrick Andrew's anguished scream on "Last Breath" to the drum-machine shuffle of "Life Goes On," was perfect. What

12. Not necessarily their best—*Set Yourself on Fire* probably wins that honor—but certainly their loveliest.

13. Wheedle-dee-duh-lee-doo.

14. Here I feel the need to add a kind of youth group disclaimer: you guys know, of course, that I would never actually do any of those things. Not drugs, anyway.

I will always remember about this record, though, is the letter to the editor of *CCM Magazine* written by a concerned listener who was disappointed that the song "Wonder Why" merely paints a picture of misery and desolation rather than pointing out that if you just believe in Jesus, everything will be cool. The editors agreed that PFR had "missed an opportunity" to point listeners in the right direction. "Wonder Why" really is a brutal song, but please keep in mind that the letter writer was concerned that a Christian band writing a Christian song for Christian listeners released on a Christian label being reviewed in a Christian magazine sold in Christian bookstores to Christian readers didn't mention Jesus enough. This is why I became bitter and cynical about Christian rock music by age sixteen.

 ## U2, *Pop* (Island, 1997)

Maybe U2 has become irrelevant, and maybe *Pop* was their first truly irrelevant album, even before they started plying their "Ok, we're sincere and earnest again, just like the *Joshua Tree*; give us money please" shtick around the turn of the century. Like most U2 records, *Pop* is full of solid, um, pop songs, with memorable melodies and pretty vocals, but its overall aesthetic sheen is purposely tacky and ugly. Pop drew attention to the ugly spectacle of pop consumerism much better than *Achtung Baby* or *Zooropa* did (they both tried), and it succeeded. It's hard to know if the whole ensuing tour was one extended ironic riff on excess, but it was ugly. This makes "Wake Up Dead Man" a particularly startling song, stark and fairly stripped of shiny overproduction. It is blasphemous and profane yet reverent. When Bono says the world is "fucked up," it's nothing we didn't already know since Genesis (the book, not the band)—what's more shocking, frankly, is the song's title and its chorus, because the "dead man" is Jesus, and for a Christian (as Bono surely is, as often as he makes his clever evasions and wears his ironic devil horns) to call Jesus a dead man is some heavy shit. This song is for all of us who live like it's Holy Saturday, which we do way too often, like Jesus really is dead and that there really is no hope and that he is not coming back, not anytime soon, not ever, and that we are alone in this fucked up world. The plea, the shout of Edge's chord after "wake up" (da na!) is the cry to shock one's own faith back into being.

10

It's Just Us and Us and Us

TO LOVE, HONOR, AND RECOMMEND RECORDS

I have a habit: I am one of those people who feels an urgent need to breathlessly share my enthusiasm for bands that are, to use the technical musical term, *awesome*. This probably comes from my father's own enthusiasm for John Coltrane and Charlie Parker; even if you have heard Parker and Coltrane a hundred times, he will pause and demand you give your full attention to one particular run or riff. It bugs me, but it has also caused me to be the kind of person who will actually turn up a Lisa Loeb song on the radio because there is one part of it that is *just so perfect*.[1]

Usually, this actually turns out ok, because enthusiasm is contagious, and sometimes people actually want to listen to the music I recommend, which is one of the reasons I keep writing about music. I find it satisfying when somebody tells me he bought a Stars album because of a review I wrote or checked out the Weakerthans because I told her about them. "Everyone has a music friend," somebody once told me. "The one person who always knows about the best new bands and can recommend something that you're sure to like." I can't think of anybody who is my music friend, so I guess I must be

---

1. "Do You Sleep"—and I really don't care if you don't like Lisa Loeb; it's awesome.

my own music friend.[2] At one time, I was so comfortable in my role as "the guy who recommends music" that I wouldn't even accept recommendations from other people—I would only give them.

Perhaps my finest moment of music friendery was when a piano-playing friend,[3] having earned his last summer paycheck from a landscaping job before going back to college, called in a favor: in exchange for letting him use my employee discount at the music store where I worked, he would let me pick out all the CDs he'd buy in his spending spree. It was the first and only time I have been given complete freedom when it comes to completely dictating what I think someone else *needs* to be listening to, and it was great. We walked brusquely through the aisles, and I loaded him up with a stack of twenty-five or thirty CDs of what were (in my mind) the best records of the era—Weezer, Lauryn Hill, Sunny Day Real Estate, Radiohead.

You might think that getting married would offer an even greater opportunity to foist my tastemaking genius on another person—finally, somebody who is stuck with me, who has to listen to my recommendations, and whose taste will eventually be shaped and molded by my thoughtful genius. Not exactly.

I married a woman with whom I share certain values and passions: a love of reading, a taste for good Southeast Asian food, a common faith, a disdain for hippies, and a mutual admiration for Sixpence None the Richer.[4] Music was an important part of our courtship, naturally, and songs neither of us had ever heard before became imbued with meaning and significance after we exchanged mixtapes—I had never really given a second thought to Rancid or Dave Matthews Band or Out of the Grey, and she'd never cared about My Bloody Valentine or Duncan Sheik.[5] We traded CDs and went to

2. I believe this scenario is also used to warn people that if you can't identify the person among your group of friends who is an insufferable jerk, it's probably you. The two roles are not so far apart, anyway.

3. The same one who later paralyzed his arm, an incident you can find elsewhere in these pages.

4. In fact, that band figures in one of the apocryphal stories about our first meeting: I seem to recall her asking me if I had a certain rare Sixpence single, which I did. She doesn't remember that, but then again, I don't remember what kind of shoes she wore at our wedding.

5. Not that she does now, necessarily. Also, if you think it is not possible for

shows together, and I counted it a joy that we both seemed to like some of the same bands. This eventually allowed us to make some money at a yard sale when we took the all-important step of merging our record collections, shedding duplicate Weezer, Sixpence, and Radiohead CDs and strengthening our love.

Things seemed to be going great, but as usual, my giddy enthusiasm for discovering new bands got in the way. I'm a faithful lover, but a fickle fan. I practice serial polygamy vis-à-vis My Favorite Band, loving two or three with all my heart at one time but moving on to newer, fresher candidates every three years or so. When I met Sarah, I had a list of five favorite bands: U2, Sixpence None the Richer, Radiohead, Weezer, and PFR. By the time I'd worked at my college's radio station for a year, many of those bands had lost their spots to Mates of State, Death Cab for Cutie, and Stars, and by the middle of the decade, the Weakerthans, Hem, and Iron & Wine were threatening to replace them.[6]

My love for these bands, I hoped, would be infectious. As the years progressed, I started freelancing for music magazines and newspapers; I lived in a magical world in which dozens of CDs arrived in the mail each week, and my new favorite band was always waiting to be discovered. I assumed I'd do what I'd done before—tell everybody I knew how awesome these new bands were, and they would all agree with me and we would happily attend concerts together and live a satisfying, harmonious life with a soundtrack provided by me. It worked with some people. It did not work with Sarah. See:

My wife hates all the music I love.

Maybe she doesn't *hate* it, but whenever I begin to really love a band, excessively love them, dangerously love them, Sarah quickly loses her patience, and it's not usually the band's fault. It's just that, like a caricature artist draws your nose longer and pointier,[7] my constant playing of albums, and listing off facts about bands, and talking about how great they are, and turning up the volume on certain parts of the

---

the same person to like My Bloody Valentine and Duncan Sheik, you are bigoted and small-minded.

6. Also, I recently started getting way into mewithoutYou. This is why I don't make lists anymore.

7. At least I assume this is what would happen if a caricaturist drew my picture; I have never wanted to see what a caricaturist would do with my nose.

songs that are especially awesome tends to accentuate those things that some might find grating or annoying. It doesn't help that I've always seen exuberance as a positive quality in an artist, and one man's exuberance tends to be one woman's obnoxious shouting.

The first time this happened was with Mates of State. I still remember the first time I heard this band, when I was a DJ at my (tiny) college radio station and their record label sent us a sampler. They were one of the first labels to indulge us like this, so we played it a lot. The song was "A Control Group," and I *could not believe how awesome*[8] *it was.* How could just two people make a song do all those things? Two vocal lines, similar in spirit but different in timbre and pitch and lyrics, wavering and snaking all over the place, creating energy *ex nihilo.* Simple drum fills punching through the thick, weird chords of the Yamaha Electone organ. It was one of the most joyous things I'd ever heard. Plus, they were a couple! How cute! Maybe my girlfriend would want to go to a show with me!

She went to the first couple of shows, but by the time Mates of State had put out two more records, Sarah was no longer coming along. Things got out of hand with "Ha Ha," which is one of the best songs I have heard in my entire life,[9] the first track from Mates of States 2003 album *Team Boo.* I found it impossible to stop listening to the song—its key and tempo changes, its relentless rhythms, its celebratory melodies. Sarah was not as impressed.

"They're just shouting," she'd say.

"That's *exuberance,*" I'd correct her.

I mostly listen to Mates of State with my headphones now.

Other bands have fallen victim to this kind of overexposure—Weezer was an early casualty. That band's early songs can be charming, even romantic, but in terms of mood-setting music, 150 bootlegged Weezer mp3s on shuffle are not something a lady wants to get down to, it seems. Most of those songs are gone from the hard drive now. There have been others cast off along the way: the Rentals, Judee Sill,

8. Perhaps you do not appreciate my overuse of *awesome*, an adjective some argue is best reserved for mountain ranges, cosmic phenomena, or God. Tough.

9. If you are not bursting with love and joy by the time they get to the "dancing all around" part, you are not human.

Soul-Junk.[10] Oftentimes when I ask Sarah what she wants to listen to, her answer is "nothing annoying." The catch-22 is, of course, that whatever I play enough of becomes annoying.

I used to despair about this. Could she not see how very important this music is to me? I have only recently gotten over my mad love affair with the Weakerthans, who are for my money simply the best, smartest, most perceptive and warm and human rock band of the last ten years. Their music has played no small part in my figuring out what is important to me in life, what my values are, and the kind of person I want to be.[11] And I'm pretty sure Sarah is sick to death of listening to them. That hurts a little, but it hurts a little more to know that I am the cause of this, that every time I play "Plea from a Cat Named Virtute" again, every time I use the word *awesome* again, I am chipping away at Sarah's musical goodwill.

Ultimately, though, I know all of that isn't very important, because being Sarah's husband has taught me that there are a lot of things more important than awesome bands. There's a wonderful scene in the British film *Brassed Off* where the curmudgeonly community brass band director finally speaks his mind: "The truth is, I thought it mattered," he says. "I thought that music mattered. But does it? Bollocks! Not compared to how people matter."

Sarah doesn't like the Danielson Famile, and I don't particularly like bananas, but I'll eat them when she buys a bunch. I also hate shopping for shoes and taking a shower in the evening instead of the morning. We all make our little sacrifices, but there are those things we can always agree upon, the nonnegotiables we will always love, like Massaman curry, Hem, and each other.

THIS MOMENTOUS GIVING

Once, when I was listening to a Christian rock record in the '90s, an alternative/grunge-era band with a song that went "SquEEEEEEEEEE-EEEEAWWWWWWWNK," my father entered the room and accused

10. To her credit, Soul-Junk's music is nearly impossible for almost everyone. I love them, but even I can barely listen to them.

11. I realize it sounds crazy to say something like this about a rock band, but then again, that's kind of the whole reason for this book.

me of listening to the musical equivalent of pornography. He was wrong, of course: the musical equivalent of pornography is smooth jazz.[12] His meaning, I think, had something to do with the sheer naked immediacy of it, the privileging of big dumb guitar feedback over chords and melody. I dismissed the comment then, but lately I cannot shake the idea that there is something to this equation of music and pornography, especially when you consider the way they have both been such driving forces on the Internet, the way they have both been commodified, distributed, and consumed in recent years.

Christians are into talking about pornography because we (rightly, I think) recognize it as a pervasive and unhealthy fact of twenty-first-century life. *Christianity Today* did a survey of Christian clergy in 2000 in which over 50 percent admitted to occasionally looking at porn Web sites. There is even a hip Christian Web site devoted to helping Christians stop looking at porn.[13]

If you are a male human who knows how to turn on a computer, you have seen Internet pornography. Porn has not saturated our society the way that music has, but the parallels are there: both are multibajillion-dollar industries built on beautiful expressions of humanity but that remake them into cheap, disposable possessions.

I started thinking again about this connection between pornography and music thanks to a Web site called MySpace, which is what people used to use before Facebook.[14] There are plenty of reasons to hate MySpace: its hideously ugly and un-user-friendly design, the great boon it is to sexual predators, its sheer vacuousness, and its being owned by Rupert Murdoch. But I'll say this: MySpace made it possible for me to be in a band with members in nearly every corner of the United States, and for people to hear our music, all via computers. In fact, without computers, the band couldn't exist: we[15] each play songs on keyboards or guitars that are plugged into laptops, send

12. In the sense that it twists and distorts a good thing, not in the sense that it is in any way titillating or exciting.

13. XXXChurch.com—really!

14. Facebook is a Web site we used to use before Twitter. If you are reading this book in the distant future, I cannot help you.

15. I say "we," but in reality, I have only contributed about fifteen to twenty seconds worth of actual music to this band because I do not know how to plug instruments into my computer.

sound files to each other, e-mail ideas for lyrics, and post the final product on the Web. MySpace is an ideal networking tool for musicians: it's one place you can go to find similar bands and potential fans, contacts for booking, and keep in touch with all of them.

It's also, apparently, an unsecure playground for hackers, who were able to log into our account (and thousands of other accounts) not long ago, changing the band picture to a pornographic photo. I logged in to delete the picture, but the next day, the hackers fought back with gusto, causing roughly fifty windows of porn to open when someone tried to visit our page. The worst (or best) part of this is that my friend Johnny, who writes most of the songs for the band, was working for a Christian nonprofit at the time. He opened the Web page in a roomful of middle-aged clergypersons, and as the dirty pictures popped up, the computer played a recorded message declaring, "HEY EVERYBODY! I'M LOOKING AT GAY PORN!"

I don't have a problem with letting the hackers "win"—we rarely used MySpace for anything important, and it's not like anybody had a vendetta against our totally unknown band in particular. Our profile was chosen nearly at random out of something like a hundred million users, and if petty-minded computer nerds think they can change the world by messing with a few people's Web sites, let them believe it. The hackers' motivation was, apparently, that they hated MySpace, and so to post a pornographic picture, a violent sexual image, was almost a literal "fuck you" to users of the Web site.

As anyone with an Internet connection knows, the pornography widely available on the Internet is hardly sexy or sensual at all; one is confronted by electronically modified images of genetically modified humans performing genital acts[16] that are anything but sexy. It's the idea of sex stripped of meaningful context. It may seem a stretch to suggest a similar problem with mp3 downloading, but Internet culture has almost turned music into something akin to pornography— files to be downloaded, possessed, consumed, and deleted when they've outlived their titillating usefulness. Music has moved from being a physical product you could own to an ephemeral digital file. Sex, it seems, has taken a different path to get to the same place. It

16. Possible name for a satirical Christian rock band.

used to be something you do; now it's something you download. They're both screwed-up iterations of what they used to be.

I remember almost to the day when I decided to stop illegally downloading music; it was the first time I saw Mates of State. They were making one hell of a joyful noise, sweaty, earnest, and beautiful, and after their performance I walked to their merchandise table to take a look. I told Jason Hammel, the drummer, that I'd enjoyed their performance. He looked exhausted and gaunt as he tried to take orders and count cash at the same time. His wife, Kori Gardner, was next to him, keeping up the same frantic pace as they had been on stage.

A lot of bands don't have an ideological problem with the idea of downloading; most independent musicians are smart enough to realize that file sharing expands their audience. I wouldn't care if somebody downloaded a song I played on—I'd just be happy they were listening. But when I saw how hard Mates of State were working, I felt ashamed that I had pulled their album off Napster. *This could be me and my wife*, I thought, struggling to make ends meet, living our dreams on a shoestring budget. *Can't I afford to pay them ten bucks?* I bought a T-shirt and made sure to do so every other time I saw the band.

But later, when Napster started to fade and mp3 blogs and YouTube made sharing music a lot more fluid and less like "stealing," I wondered, *shouldn't music, like sex, be a free and joyful exchange of intimacy?*[17] Maybe, but the important thing seems to be that while the Internet changed the way we could enjoy and experience music and relationships, it also screwed up all that stuff a little; the Internet now seems to be a distraction from a life lived in community, a vision of music or sex or anything that is grounded in honest-to-goodness, sweaty, energetic human contact. I guess I'm learning that I don't get a meaningful music scene from downloading files anymore than I can get meaningful sex from a porn site.

You can still find Mates of State songs on the Internet, of course, but they tour nonstop, making music in front of people, selling albums, supporting themselves, meeting people, making a living for themselves and their family—they have two daughters now, and in

17. In a different way, obviously, unless maybe you are Diana Krall and Elvis Costello, but I don't really want to think about that.

fact, they mentioned in an interview that their first was conceived backstage at a show. Actually, I think that is wonderful. I will take that over MySpace any day.

Wendell Berry, my favorite poet-farmer-philosopher, writes in one of his classic essays of marriage and sex: "If they had only themselves to consider, lovers would not need to marry, but they must think of others and of other things. They say their vows to the community as much as to one another, and the community gathers around them to hear and to wish them well, on their behalf and its own."[18] I'm reminded of this when I think of some couples I'm close to: how Dave and Anna's wedding was put together by a small army of devoted friends and family at minimal cost, the way Nathan wrote Ben Folds a letter asking him to dedicate "The Luckiest" to Christy at a concert (Folds did), the way Roy and Lucy let us live in their basement for a summer. If music matters because people matter, I figure there must be a way to get to a place where marriage and music come together in an outward explosion of love and community, something that I believe can only be sustained by God.

When we were first married, Sarah and I shared a house with two roommates and a couple of rock bands. We didn't know anyone in our neighborhood very well and we felt a little guilty that the bands playing in the basement were (probably) causing everyone grief, what with playing loud, distorted music badly, so we decided to invite the whole neighborhood, anybody who lived within earshot, over for a potluck and concert in the backyard. Our across-the-street neighbors, who had lived on the block for fifteen years, told us that this was the first time anyone had ever tried to get the neighborhood together. Why did we do it? Probably from being literal about Jesus's talk about loving your neighbor,[19] but also, I think and I hope, as an extension of the love we had for each other. We were newlyweds, we had jobs and lives we liked, a home we wanted to open, and a lot of love and music to go around, so we invited the neighborhood to

18. Berry, *Sex, Economy, Freedom & Community* (New York: Pantheon, 1993) 137–38.

19. Who says you have to be a humorless fundie to take the Bible "literally"?

share it all. My band Team November played in the backyard, and I felt like, instead of being a nuisance, we were giving something to our neighbors.

As Berry continues, "Here, at the heart of community life, we find not something to sell as in the public market but this momentous giving."[20] If you ask me, the whole universe is a momentous giving. From pop songs to planets, God gives and gives and gives, and to be a tiny part of that by playing a free backyard concert and barbeque feels supremely, blissfully right.

This Wendell Berry stuff is great, but you are only climbing into bed with one person at the end of the day,[21] and music does not only open one outward to the world, but can also send one quickly back to the arms of one's beloved. One of the only times I have undertaken a remotely journalist-like writing assignment took me to a dingy dance club in Shanghai, a former bomb shelter that had become the city's hippest venue for expats and Chinese yuppies with international aspirations. I was there to see a DJ called James Pants, who I'd gone to college with for a while years before, and to report on what happened when scattershot postmodern hip-hop made its way past the Bamboo Curtain. I met a lot of interesting people and got a couple of free drinks, but by the end of the night there was only one thing on my mind: how can anybody live in this city? Or perhaps more accurately, how can anybody live this life? I left the concert at two in the morning and it was still going strong, and getting stronger. The place was packed with people who wanted to be seen looking cool, or aloof, or sexy, or in some cases, very, very drunk.

The first truly bonkers moment was when James played Daft Punk's high-energy dance-party track "One More Time." Instantly, two thirds of the people in attendance started making a sort of demonstrative pointing gesture that is internationally acknowledged as the "Hell *yes*, this is my *jam*" signal. It was everybody's jam. I looked out at the sea of people and the tiny worlds they inhabited, their

20. Berry, 138.

21. At least that's what I assume. We don't really have time or space to go into it if you're not.

gauzy gazes zeroing in, sharklike, on the people they were hoping to ensnare. One curvy, dark-haired girl (a white girl, a "foreigner," as we quickly learn to call even each other in China) caught my eye and smiled a wide, inviting smile, the kind of smile I had never before been on the receiving end of, the kind of smile that I think ends with breakfast. It caught me completely by surprise, disoriented me like a tranquilizer dart—until James came to the rescue and dropped the needle on the Beach Boys' "Don't Worry Baby." Immediately I was snapped back to reality, and I saw my sleeping wife at home, thought of how warm her body must be and how the place I most want to be at two in the morning is not a dark basement with two hundred strangers listening to dance music, but curled around Sarah, forever and ever until we wake up.

FIVE ALBUMS I LOVE THAT MY WIFE MAY OR MAY NOT LOVE

 Mates of State, *Our Constant Concern* (Polyvinyl, 2002)

This may not be the best Mates record (that is either *Team Boo*, which is the perfect distillation of their organ-drums shtick, or *Re-Arrange Us*, their first ambitious fleshed-out-with-other-instruments record), but it is the most vibrant—the organ is all up in your business, the vocals are belted with abandon, and the songs really sound like the breathless rush of married people's conversations, which they are. The music twists and turns as Gardner and Hammel talk over each other, sometimes at cross-purposes, sometimes complementary, yet always creating something beautiful together. The highlight is "Über Legitimate," a song they played at their own wedding, which would be disgustingly sweet if it weren't so solid and muscular— their paean to love is not cutesy-wootsy; they refer to their union as "something static and solemnly invincible." Amen to that, but the great thing is that a few tracks later, they get into a musical fight on "A Duel Will Settle This." That is some realistic domesticity. Plus, the one time I interviewed Mates of State, they were on different phone extensions and Hammel was doing the dishes. Even if you don't like their music, Sarah, you've got to admire that.

Hem, *Eveningland* (Rounder, 2004)

I could go (and have gone) on and on about Hem, who showed up at just the time I needed to know that contemporary pop music could be gentle and life-affirming instead of trendy and brash and ugly. I love this band like they were family, and *Eveningland* has a lot to say about love and family, from "The Fire Thief," which is sung to a sleeping child, to "Strays," which is one of the best songs about marriage I have ever heard. Without giving too much away,[22] the song makes a case for marriage that is more than the unity of two individuals—that it is maybe about whole communities of people, whole towns—and it does this so subtly, barely mentioning marriage at all except for the solemn, quiet repetition of "I do" during the bridge. Since we've been married, Hem is the first band that Sarah and I have agreed on and both have the same amount of love for. That alone is worth celebrating.

Zero Seven, *Simple Things* (Palm, 2001)

Like Hem, Zero 7 is a band Sarah introduced me to thanks to her internship at a Seattle music magazine and its concomitant avalanche of freebies. She brought home this, the first Zero 7 album, from the office one day, and I was immediately smitten by the way it blends elements of what people tend to think of as "electronica" with actual classy songwriting and supersexy vocals. We saw Zero 7 (again for free—do you hate us yet?) a few years later at a sit-down theater, and although the band's blonde female singer looked giddy and stoned the whole time, the ecstatic throaty passion of her vocals, combined with the slick bedroom funk of the band, was pure sexuliciousness. I gave this record to my friend Dave when he married my friend Anna, and within a year they had made a baby. This is not a coincidence. I also made sure that I brought it with me to our overpriced honeymoon suite, which I made sure was equipped with a CD player ahead of time. Their subsequent records deviate a little bit from the main musical message[23] of this one, so keep it simple. You know what you have to do.[24]

---

22. Without quoting the lyrics at all, in fact, because it will cost too much money.

23. "Let's do it."

24. In the context of a loving, monogamous marriage, obviously.

The Weakerthans, *Reconstruction Site* (Epitaph, 2003)

I wish I hadn't overplayed this one. *Reconstruction Site* is an elegant pop-punk record lovingly crafted by an incredibly smart, literate, and punchy power-pop band from Winnipeg, Manitoba. Their songs are compassionate, careful portraits of people who *believe* in things, even when those beliefs are frustrated, like on the short and bittersweet "Hospital Vespers" and the feline pep talk (seriously) of "Plea from a Cat Named Virtute." All Weakerthans records tend to focus on small things, the personal and local, but *Reconstruction Site* also includes a loving *apologia* for grand narratives of belief in "Our Retired Explorer (Dines with Michel Foucault in Paris, 1961)," in which an Antarctic voyager, after a dinner with the incomprehensible philosopher, decides to hightail it back to the ice, sure of his dedication to the frozen continent. It's just three dumb chords, but suddenly God is an iceberg.

The first mixtape Sarah made for me

This is not the kind of thing you do after you're married—if you live together, you don't need to hang on to a physical/musical object to remind yourself of your lover—but one of my favorite recordings of the last decade is the first mixtape Sarah made for me, right after we started dating, while everything was still fresh and exciting and we were still skinny and mostly interested in making out in the dorm stairwell. For various reasons, I will not publicly admit that there are songs by Out of the Grey, the Aquabats, and Dave Matthews Band that I really like on this tape. But I know every song is a piece of her from before she met me, before I started shoving CDs in her face and shouting "LISTEN TO THIS!" and I love this compilation for that reason. This first mixtape you get[25] from a new lover is one of the most pure and true things you will ever receive, and you must treasure it. I played this tape in the car for years, even after we were married.

25. Or, I should say, *got*—you poor, poor children of today.

11

All the Way to China

LET'S GET OUT OF THIS COUNTRY

I spent my early twenties turning myself into a comfortable West Coast urban-dweller and frequenter of independent coffee shops and rock shows, with a job of modest upward mobility. Moving to China didn't seem to have anything to do with the life trajectory I'd been planning. The move to Seattle for college, getting a job in a "helping"-related field (fund-raising for a Catholic social services organization), playing in a band—these each seemed like logical next steps. Getting married, buying a house, and starting a family were next on the list. Some of my friends got married before they were finished with college—my own *parents* got married before they finished college, and my father had been in his job, a real career-type job, for eight years by the time he was the age I am now. Life in Seattle was great. My band was there, I could go to concerts all the time, my wife had a cool job at a magazine that got us free tickets to stuff, and we had a church that we liked. We even had a Netflix subscription.

Then we suddenly started talking about moving away. Far, far away.

Sarah comes from a long line of movers. Her grandparents left China for Wales and Malaysia, which her parents left for England and the United States. She has relatives on most continents and a niece who can accurately be described as Chinese-Malaysian-Welsh-

American-Irish. If it weren't for Sarah, I don't think I would have ever realized that (with a few notable exceptions) if you want to live someplace else in the world, any place, you can just go there. You can just *move*. She was keen to do so, but I had never imagined moving away from Seattle—why would I want to leave the place I had always wanted to move *to*? True, I had been daydreaming about getting into a different career, something with more reading and writing and no data entry, but Seattle seemed as good a place as any to pursue that, and it didn't seem like leaving was a good move.

I'd been avoiding Sarah's comments and questions about moving abroad, maybe to teach English or to do some volunteer work. She talked seriously about it, and I grunted vaguely positive responses. "Sounds interesting," I'd say. "That would be cool." But I didn't have any intention to leave the Pacific Northwest. Sarah was persistent, though, and the idea was on the table; it was a decision that would have to be made: we could either keep living in Seattle forever, or we could move away to some crazy place we had never been to before.

After a concert at the Showbox (Seattle's biggest and best rock venue at the time), Sarah and I were having a drink at a restaurant on Seattle's First Avenue, and she wasn't going to let me evade her questions any more. Did I want to move or not? I was unsure about this idea of joining a volunteer organization. What if they send us to Bangladesh, where there's all kinds of violence? Or Mongolia, where everything is so isolated and cold, and they drink fermented horse milk and tear your arms out of your sockets if you refuse to drink it?[1] What about the drug lords in South America? The unstable government in Thailand? The pollution in China?

Sarah looked at me with a rare flash of anger. "What are you so afraid of?" she demanded.

I almost felt as if I couldn't move after hearing that question. *Fear* was something I had never really considered to be part of my life, but it was clearly, now, the problem. We'd just been to see a band called the Fire Theft, an indie rock group made up of members from the pioneering "emo" (whatever that is) band Sunny Day Real Estate. Their last song, "Sinatra," was this haunting epic with a lyric that stuck with me: "There is no freedom in life without freedom of

---

1. Obviously, this is not entirely true, but that's how I felt at the time.

mind." The song is about maturity, deciding to become a grown-up. It's about the tension between grand, youthful idealism and the truth that getting on with things like family and work and worship is not actually a bad way to go at all.

"What are you so afraid of losing?" she asked.

Everything. I was afraid of losing the life I had built for myself, the life I thought I wanted, the one in which my greatest joy was walking up and down University Avenue after getting a paycheck, hitting every used CD shop on each side of the street, and scouring the one-dollar bins for hours, coming home with a stack of ten new albums that would soon become a part of me. The one where I got to play rock shows with my childhood heroes (early that year, Jesse Sprinkle, the drummer from Poor Old Lu, had borrowed *my drums* during a show we played together!), interview my favorite bands, and eat at a variety of inexpensive Thai and Indian restaurants two or three times a week.

Our house was filled with shelves of books, records, and DVDs I'd bought, believing, with John Cusack's Rob Gordon in the film *High Fidelity*, that "these things matter." And sure, they matter some, they mean something, but *why*? Because they're cool? Because they make me feel cool? I didn't seem to have that freedom of mind the Fire Theft was singing about. I was too in love with my life to see that everything I had ever wanted might not actually be all that the world had to offer.

I knew I wasn't going to stop loving those things, but I felt stupid for wanting them more than anything else.

I looked down at my pint for a while before returning my wife's gaze. What was I afraid of losing?

"Nothing," I finally said.

And we moved to China.

AMAZING GRACE, HOW STRANGE THE SOUND

Americans who "know a lot" about Eastern culture bug the hell out of me. We think that because we know the difference between *tom kha gai* and *pad see ew* and because we know that Koreans use metal

chopsticks, we have somehow plumbed the depths of Oriental in-
scrutability.[2] Even though I lived in China for two years, and after
leaving, moved to one of the most Chinese cities in North America to
do research about education in China, I try very hard not to make any
grand pronouncements on the subject of Things I Know about China,
because I know very, very little. I cannot read or write Chinese, can
barely speak it, and constantly second-guess my behavior when I am
in China, as I inevitably do or say the impolite thing whenever I'm in
a sensitive social situation. I am hyperaware of all this because I am
a white man married to an Asian American woman, and I am afraid
that any time a white guy puts on a patronizing kindergarten-teacher
voice to tell an Asian woman she has "*very* good English" in the hopes
that she will sleep with him, I will be guilty by association.

Still, there are certain stereotypical statements I find myself making about China and its people simply out of convenience. This kind
of nationality-based shorthand works well in China, where *who* is
known for *what* is usually quite clearly delineated. Everybody's home-
town, for example, is the world capital of something. One town may
be the home of the world's biggest zipper factory. Another has the
best fried rice in the country. Another has the best orange trees. This
extends to countries, too: British people are "gentlemen," Americans
are "energetic," Chinese are "hard-working," and Thailand has a lot
of transsexuals. As much as I didn't want to play into stereotypes—
I refused repeated requests to "sing a song" and thereby prove my
students' hunch that foreigners love attention, being loud, singing,
dancing, and music—I was still *me*, and I couldn't escape the reality
that I am, in fact, deeply preoccupied with popular music.

I wondered, when we moved, whether my obsession with music
would move with us, or if it would be something I'd leave behind
with my CD collection.[3] What kind of musical culture would there be
in China for me to be a part of? It wasn't going to be like our sojourn
in California, where we lived before moving to China. There had
been some culture shock to deal with when we arrived in the Golden

2. This is sarcasm, but did you notice how I'm dropping little hints that I
actually *do* know a lot of this stuff? Which is, like, way worse.

3. Though, to my eternal gratefulness, Sarah spent the two weeks before our
move burning around seven hundred CDs to our computer, so we were able to
continue feeding our ears and souls with the bands we loved.

State—they had a lot more hippies than Washington State, and everything was more expensive—but life in northern California turned out to be pretty similar to what we knew in Seattle. There were still friends to drink beers and complain about American Christianity with. There were jobs, churches, bookstores, and concert venues. There was no guarantee we'd encounter such similarities in China.

I had no plans to abandon my quest to mix what you might call disposable pop culture (i.e., rock music) with steadfast religious conviction (i.e., Christianity). And in fact, I found that something of this same mixture happens in China, too. It's a society that has deep roots in religion and philosophy, but which is growing and changing so quickly that half the time it seems like everyone is making up life as they go along. Unlike my own Foursquare-inspired remix of fundie faith and passionate pop, however, China's sacred/secular mash-up emerges when Confucian/Buddhist/Taoist belief meets the modern-day gospel of economic development. There's not a whole lot of Jesus in there.

That's what I thought, anyway. On my very first day of teaching, though, it was clear that the rock-and-faith mix I'd always known had followed me around the world. I played a Sigur Rós song for my writing students and asked them to freewrite anything that came to mind upon hearing the wordless coos. One student wrote, "The low sound of the piano makes me feel calm and feel the paradise of the church, as if I were getting much closer to the Christ and understood the great suffering of his death and the great sanity of his coming back to life."

"The Christ?" Here?

I later found out that not a small number of my students were Christians—certainly a much smaller number than at the Christian university I went to, but a lot more than I'd have thought. Staunch devotion to communism is no longer the only game in town in China. In fact, the idea that religion is unheard of in the country is far from the truth: something like one-third of Chinese people (which is equivalent to the entire population of the United States), according to a Pew study, practice some form of religion. Sadly, I didn't pursue any kind of fellowship with my Christian students, because that's the kind of thing that can get a foreign teacher fired— there are vaguely worded laws about what visitors to the country can and can't do when it comes to religion. So, whether out of cowardice or obedience, I didn't push my luck.

I was walking on eggshells when I taught on Christmas day itself (their version of "Christmas break" is in January), but I thought I should say something about the holiday. All my students knew what Christmas was—there were Santa Clauses everywhere—so I explained the meaning of the English word *secular* and that Christmas was both a secular and religious holiday. I started getting nervous when I tried to explain the religious part of Christmas, stammering out Christian History for Dummies: "See, there were these people called the Jews— you know the Jews?" (A few did.) "So, they believed in God, and they were waiting for God to send someone to save them, and then this guy Jesus was born, and some of them believed that he was the one who would save them, but some of them didn't, and so now, uh, this might sound weird, but now there was this new religion called Christianity—you know Christianity?"

I certainly wasn't proselytizing, but it was perhaps the first time in my life I had ever done what evangelicalism is all about: telling people about Jesus. It's just what all the Christian magazines, bands, radio stations, and youth groups of my younger years had been telling me I should do. I wasn't preaching, exactly, I was just saying that there were these people who believed in God, and there was this guy Jesus who they thought could save people, and I was one of these people. That was about as far as we got. My faith may be rooted in evangelicalism, but I'm not an evangelist.

After class, I stayed behind to erase the chalkboards, now a mess of diagrams and words: "Jews," "Santa Claus," "Jesus," "secular," "apples,"[4] "Christianity." One of my more outgoing students lingered at the door.

"Joel, I want to give you a Christmas present," she said.

I had two immediate reactions: (a) *Sweet, I always knew being a teacher totally paid off vis-à-vis getting free swag from students*; and (b) *Oh crap, I'm alone with a female student and this is going to turn weird, and I'm going to be accused of sexual harassment and be deported.*

---

4. In China, you give people apples on Christmas. It has something to do with a pun on the Chinese word for *apple*, but I can't really explain it.

"I'll walk with you," she said as we left the classroom. Suddenly, she started to sing, with a voice whose purity shocked me out of my post-teaching sluggishness as it echoed through the hallway. *"Qiyi endian, hedeng gantian . . ."*

It was "Amazing Grace." She finished the verse and said, very sincerely, "I want you to know that even though you are far away from your friends and family this Christmas, God is with you, and Jesus always loves you."

I swallowed the lump in my throat and thanked her as we prepared to go our separate ways.

"Joel, our pastor told us that nowadays in the West, the young people don't believe in God. Is that true?" she asked.

"Yeah, I guess so," I said. "A lot of people don't."

"But why?"

What could I say to this? How could I even begin to unravel the unholy melting pot of scientism, postmodernity, religion, self-reliance, belief, and unbelief that swirls around my country of origin?

"I don't know. I guess maybe when people think they have everything they want, they feel like they don't need God."

I thanked the student again for her song and rode my bike home. But I might have been wrong about that answer. I was playing to some kind of stereotype, where people in "the West" are decadent and have turned their backs on God, while those lucky poor people in the not-West still have some kind of magical childlike ability to believe in God, and aren't they cute? That's not really true, especially not in China. Does having all your human needs and wants met mean you don't need God?

The sun was shining, and waiting at home was a stack of pirated DVDs to watch on the couch and a cache of Christmas goodies to eat. I was heading home to celebrate with my wife, and my student was going to celebrate with the Christian students she called her "brothers and sisters." We had all we needed, I'm sure. But we were both proof that the other's stereotype was wrong: she, the godless communist, indoctrinated with atheism; me, the decadent Westerner, soul deadened by money and gluttony. Perhaps we do each face unique challenges to our own belief, but we share a faith, and we shared a song.

THE ABSOLUTELY TRUE STORY OF MY FAILED ATTEMPT
TO JOIN A CHINESE DEATH METAL BAND

When we decided to move, I wasn't sure how I'd navigate living in such a "foreign" culture, but I knew that there was rock music in China, and I was determined to get as involved in it as I could, which is not a lot, it turns out, when you have the vocabulary of a three-year-old. It doesn't help that Chinese people are, as a rule, very polite to foreigners, so if you are able to say something like "Thank you" to a waitress, or "Please don't stick that Q-tip so far into my ear" to a barber, you will invariably be met with some variation of "Wow, your Chinese is so good!" In other contexts, this might be patronizing, but in China it's both a compliment and a deterrent for language learning—I don't need to study if everyone is telling me how great I am at Chinese.

Unfortunately, it's easy to start believing these lies about yourself—that you, as a foreign guest, are special and that the country you are in is lucky to have you. You even get the idea that maybe you will become famous. China is a country that has a TV show called *Foreigners Sing Chinese Songs*, so pale-faced fame is ripe for the taking. I considered myself somehow above that. Instead, I decided to audition for a death metal band.

Joining a Chinese metal band was perhaps one of the worst ideas I have ever had, for many reasons. First, I have never really enjoyed metal, unless you count the last forty-five seconds or so of "Lint of Love" by Cibo Matto, where Sean Lennon comes in with a chugging metal riff on the bass. In fact, I have never actually listened to metal at all except for looking up a YouTube video of Slayer so I could understand John Darnielle's book *Reign in Blood*, which is based on an album by that band. On the whole, I find the genre unpleasant.

Also, the band was looking for a bass player, and not only had I not played the bass for about two years, but I also did not have a bass guitar with me in China and was therefore unable to practice the one song the band had a recording of. Plus, there was the language thing, and the fact that I was too honest with the band to make them very confident about my fit for the band: "I don't really listen to metal, but I think it could be interesting," was the best I could muster.

The only thing I had going for me was that, as far as I could tell, I would only be required to play one very low note,[5] over and over, if I joined this band. Most of the technical skill would be handled by the drummer, a Japanese guy who worked as a salesman for a well-known drum manufacturer and therefore had about five hundred cymbals, and the guitarist, who was the only person I met in China who actually had a so-called Fu Manchu mustache or long metal-band hair. (I met other people in metal bands, including a kid who played in a band called Death God, but even with a badass name like that, the band members looked like office clerks). The band's singer was a soft-spoken woman who had recently changed her English name from Lisa to Monica. (This happens frequently in China, especially with college students. At the beginning of every semester, I'd get messages like "I'm changing my English name to Jessica," which is fine, or really bizarre ones, like "I'm changing my English name from Commander to Rainbow."[6])

Lisa–Monica, who worked as a mild-mannered assistant for a PR firm by day, had completely mastered a vocal style I would call "really, really scary and evil, especially considering that it is coming from a small Chinese woman and not a three-hundred-pound white guy with satanic tattoos." Her guttural growls were another reason I started thinking the band was maybe not the best fit for me. Lisa–Monica and I had a conversation via instant messaging the day before I was to come to the audition, and I desperately tried to find some common ground.

> Me: How about screamo? Do you guys like screamo? (*remembering that it actually has some melody*).
> Lisa–Monica: Not really. We listen to thrash and metalcore.
> Me (*trying not to admit that I don't know what those are*): Ok. Well, do you do any singing?
> Lisa–Monica: I sing a little, but it's mostly screaming.
> Me: I see.

I showed up for the audition dressed like a prep-school English teacher, which is not something I recommend, fashionwise, for a

---

5. E, obviously.
6. Those are real English names I heard in China. Also, "Baby Parrot."

metal band audition. Everyone else was wearing black metal T-shirts. The band rocked, but I had trouble figuring out what exactly I was supposed to do. They asked me to jam with the drummer so they could hear me play, so I drew on my extensive knowledge of '90s alt-rock bass lines in the hopes that nobody would notice I was not spontaneously being creative, just playing Spacehog's "In the Meantime." I left the audition assuming that they'd realized I was not the best choice for a bassist, but holding out hope that they might give me a callback out of desperation.

Soon after the audition, I found a music school that was a fifteen-minute bike ride north of our apartment where, for about $2.50 an hour, I could bash away on a crappy drum set in a tiny soundproof room. It was awful on my ears, but for an hour every Saturday morning, I got to pretend I was the drummer for Ben Folds Five or me-withoutYou or Sunny Day Real Estate, and everything that was stuck in my soul, all the negativity and anxiety and fear, was surrendered with sacramental physicality. It became a weekly ritual, the closest I'd get to God and to being in a band most weeks. I'm back in North America now, where I go to church every Sunday, but every time I feel like there is a closed fist at the center of my solar plexus, I wish that room was still a bike ride away.

Not long after I discovered the drum room, I got an e-mail from Lisa–Monica. "You're a really good bass player," she wrote, somewhat flatteringly, "but you are not fit for metal, just as I am not fit for country music." She was right. Even though I'd made something of a life for myself in a country that is the epitome of *foreign*, even though I felt confident enough to argue over the price of a DVD and order and eat a spicy duck's head, I was never meant to be in a death metal band.

FIVE ALBUMS TO LISTEN TO ON A CROSS-CULTURAL JAUNT ACROSS THE GLOBE

 Sigur Rós, *( )* (PIAS/Fat Cat, 2002)

I agree with my student: there is something that feels inherently divine about this music—its epic scope, its gravitas, its gentleness and wrath. Really, any Sigur Rós album would do, but *( )* was the first that really emphasized openness. The title, a pair of parentheses with nothing inside, invites you to fill the empty space yourself. The liner notes, translucent, blank pages, can be scribbled on if you want (the band said as much in interviews). And most importantly, the lyrics are just a series of meaningless syllables. The mostly instrumental songs are full of space, but they are so beautiful; track two is still the only instrumental music that has moved me to tears when I heard it in concert. You fill in the meaning and make it a worship experience if you want. Maybe the Holy Spirit can fill in the rest.

Sunny Day Real Estate, *How It Feels to Be Something On* (Sub Pop, 1998)

I never really have any idea what Jeremy Enigk is talking about, but that doesn't mean I don't love him. The abovementioned Fire Theft record was the first time he made relatively plain statements about things like God and girls. When I interviewed him, he attributed Sunny Day's lyrical haze to Dan Hoerner, or at least to the fact that they wrote the songs together. More often than not, on their first couple of records it just sounds like they're making stuff up off the top of their heads—I defy you to explain what the words "Pheurton Skeurto," "Snibe," and "J'Nuh" even mean, let alone what those songs are about. But on *How It Feels* there is just enough of the stuff of real life to sink your teeth into. "Guitar and Video Games" evokes a painful nostalgia for simpler times when you didn't have student loans or babies, when all you did was play those things, eat Doritos, and love life. Even the title song, which never really gets beyond its final preposition—how it feels to be something on *what*, exactly?—captures some kind of joyous life force in its pounding chorus.

Lonely China Day, *Sorrow* (Tag Team, 2007)

I bought as many Chinese indie rock albums as I could when I was in China, and not all of them were good. It's become a kind of cliché for Americans to discover some relatively Western cultural trend in China—music, food, wine, golf, religion—and explain how the way they do it is weird and equivalent to how Americans used to do it fifty years ago but that they'll eventually figure it out and rule over us all. Obviously, that's wrong, but the earnest mediocrity of Chinese indie rock almost had me ready to believe this until I saw Lonely China Day. They're a post-rock band in the sense that their songs are long and unfold gradually. The songs of frontman Deng Pei don't feel dangerous or experimental, but their structures are unconventional enough—the verses and choruses don't seem as important as moods—to lend some credence to what music critic Yan Jun once wrote about Chinese music: "To speak of 'experimentation' in China means to discuss it literally: every single person in the entire country experiments daily and tries out new things. . . . While Westerners believe that the Chinese are re-inventing sounds that already exist, the Chinese believe that they are simply re-inventing themselves."

 ## Cibo Matto, *Stereo Type A* (Warner Bros., 1999)

To admit that I love Cibo Matto once again forces me to walk the line of Orientalism I want so much to avoid. Maybe when I first discovered them I did have a creepy white-boy crush on Miho Hatori, but that was only because I did not know any better. Cibo Matto is not a cutesy Japanese girl group; they are instead the greatest pop band of the '90s. Their debut, *Viva la Woman*, is a good record—it is much deeper than the novelty-ish singles "Birthday Cake" and "Know Your Chicken" would suggest—but their second (and final) album, *Stereo Type A*, is a flat-out masterpiece. I don't know any other band that can blend genres so seamlessly—rap, bossa nova, metal, dance, rock, what have you—without sounding forced. It all flows so naturally because, you can tell, Hatori and Yuka Honda have a deep knowledge and respect for all music. When I am not sure who I am or what I'm doing, there is one line from this record that always snaps me back to reality: "Where's your identity?" I don't always have the same answer to that question, but it is a question that always needs to be asked.

 ## Ben Folds Five, *The Unauthorized Biography of Reinhold Messner* (Sony/550 Music, 1999)

I got into a disagreement with a drunk guy at a friend's wedding about which Ben Folds Five album is the best. "*Reinhold Messner*, that's an album," he grunted, swaying gently toward me, "but *Whatever and Ever Amen*, that's a career. A *career*." Both albums are excellent, but the heft and weight of *Reinhold Messner*, for me, launch it far above its looser and sloppier (in a good way) predecessor. Folds has touched on faith in his solo work (notably in songs like "Not the Same" and "Jesusland"), but the care with which human predicaments are articulated on this record marks it as much a work of theology and philosophy as a pop opus. From the epic anguish of "Narcolepsy," which is about the dull pain of living without intention ("I'm not tired / I just sleep"), the whole album is a map of life's dark places. Yet it ends with rest ("Lullabye") and a glimmer of hope: "The world has more for you than it seems . . ."

12

Soon I'll Be Thirty

I DON'T WANT TO BE THIRTY

I had a plan to engineer my life in such a way that it would make for a great final chapter in a book. Ideally, by the time I had to write the part that would become the last few pages, things would be looking up. The plan was that, after moving to Canada,[1] we'd find a great church, settle in, and make friends with whom we could share meals and CDs. I would also figure out a way to make my career as an English language teacher and researcher mesh with my other great passions, writing and music, and I'd start building a body of work that combined all those things.[2] I would meet like-minded Christians—friends who would never listen to K-LOVE but who know that God shows up in rock & roll—and start a band influenced by David Axelrod, the Prayer Chain, and mewithoutYou. The final scene could even be the first gig with my new band. The book would come out on my thirtieth birthday, whereupon my wife would announce that she was pregnant and I would be offered a lucrative job that allowed us to split our time between the Pacific Northwest and China.

None of this, of course, has happened.

1. Oh yeah, by the way, I moved to Canada.
2. This wasn't all that well thought out. What exactly am I going to write about? Christian bands who sing in English as a Second Language?

As book deadlines whizzed by, I became disappointed, depressed even, that I had not gotten all these ducks in any sort of row. I wanted every area of my life to be finally working out. I wanted clarity and coherence, freedom from the muddling that characterized most of my twenties. Instead, I am learning to embrace a more robust muddling. What actually happened is this:

I posted an ad online trying to start a band, a very specific kind of band, with a list of influences (see above) and an agenda (rearranging old hymns) so specific that they precluded almost anyone from responding. I got only one response, from a guy whose name kept changing every time he e-mailed me. When I asked him if he was familiar with the influences I had named, he said he'd once known a homeless banjo player who might be interested, except that he had left town recently.

I did join a band, but not the kind I'd dreamed of. On idle weeknights, I found myself browsing the Craigslist musicians' section, first typing in the names of my favorite bands (Weakerthans, Weezer, Stars, Sigur Rós), then specific positions bands were looking to fill ("drummer needed," "looking for bassist"), and finally, on the off-chance that there were other religious people who wanted to play chaotic post-rock, words like *Christian*, *church*, and *Jesus*. It was through this final search that I found a band I recently started playing drums with, not because anybody in it is religious, as far as I know, but because one of their influences is the Jesus and Mary Chain. A spate of other shoegazing bands mentioned in the ad was enough to prompt me to answer—I've been obsessed with the shimmering, echoey pop songs of Ride recently—and we may even have a gig at a local music festival coming up. Playing with a new group of people you've never met is a tentative thing, a step of faith, even, but so far things are working.

We tried a couple of churches: one big, shiny one whose neo-Calvinism left me angry on the drive home, and one small, tight-knit one whose genuinely kind members suggested we might want to try a different church, because if we stayed with them we would probably end up leaving anyway. I even fantasized about converting to Catholicism or the Anglican Church, but I haven't come anywhere close, except attending an Ash Wednesday Mass. Finally, we decided to tentatively plant ourselves in a church very similar to those I have gone to for most of my life, churches that follow the old worship-service formula of songs, sermon, and some awkward standing around with coffee. There have been no epiphanies, no sudden feelings of being home, and often I find the actual churchgoing awkward and wonder why I'm there. We've joined something that, depending on who you are, you might know as a "small group," "cell group," "Bible study," or "home group," with people we are slowly beginning to know and love. These things take time.

One of the first CDs my parents ever owned—in fact, I think they had to go out and buy a CD player in order to play it—is *Bargainville*, the first album by the obscure Canadian vocal group Moxy Früvous. It was among the first pop albums I listened to after I became absorbed in music, and it is imprinted on my heart in the way Simon and Garfunkel's *Concert in Central Park* and Sixpence None the Richers' *The Fatherless and the Widow* are. There's a line on that record, about the ambivalence one feels upon turning thirty, that I could not fathom at the time I first heard it, but repeats, often, in my head these days: "I've got some big plans / Goodwill has some big hands."

I'm about to turn thirty, which seems like the beginning of the end of life as I know it; as my friend Nathan says, thirty is the twelve of adulthood. There's a tension in those Moxy Früvous lines that I feel more acutely now—I don't particularly want to be thirty. I feel anxious about my career, confused about my theology, and scared of getting older and losing my hearing without even having gone on tour with a band. But these fears are making me see how much I need those things I have always needed. I hold my favorite bands more tightly now—there are fewer of them—because I see how rare it is to find a group of people who love each other and the world enough to put the necessary energy into making beautiful music. I treasure my belief in God as I poke around for a new theology, because I feel that to believe anything else, to abandon this story I live in, would be a failure of imagination of the highest order.

And who knows what might happen? I'm sure I'll settle into a job I'm happy with soon enough. This new band might make a great record and go on tour. My new church might be one I stay in forever.

I might become Anglican or get way into opera. I might write some books. I might have some kids. I might start to better understand why I am a Christian and what to do about it.

I don't know what comes after thirty but I do believe Goodwill has some big hands.

AND YOU GIVE YOURSELF AWAY

I am still recovering from the fallout of a time when "Christian music" sometimes seemed shorthand for "manipulative inauthenticity." But I am really, really happy about what is happening with Christian-faith-based music. My friend Zadok, who has made a string of amazing recordings that marry the grandeur of post-rock and chamber music with the intimate emotionalism of indie rock and the solemnity of high-church liturgy, put it this way when I told him a band I was writing about: "Do they prefer Jesus?" He was joking, but that's how much we tiptoe around the cultural minefield laid for us by CCM.

I feel that the idea of "Christian rock," except as an accessory to church events, is disappearing and that the idea of guitar-bass-drums music as a way to express your faith seems more relevant than ever. Even people who don't identify themselves as Christians are wrestling with the implications and iconography of faith and God and redemption in their music. I have been heartened in the last decade by artists like Iron & Wine, Arcade Fire, Stars, Kanye West, Jurassic Five, the Weakerthans, and Bright Eyes, to name a scant few. And I feel like the fight for whatever is true, noble, pure, lovely, admirable, excellent, and praiseworthy in popular music just might be won, or at least that it's a fair fight—that cheap disposability and cynical nonsense, like the horrible Nickelback video I just watched while trying not to write, won't win the day.

But what I am worried about is that even as this development means more opportunities to root around in the dark corners of my faith, the music no longer pulls me out of myself. Especially since I started writing about it, especially since Napster and MySpace and YouTube and Twitter became the medium for sharing, listening to, and talking about it, music has felt less and less human to me.

I remember almost every CD I ever bought—what day it was, what the weather was like, who I was with. I remember holding My Bloody Valentine's *Loveless* in my hands as I sat in a now-bankrupt big box store and listened as those first four snare hits and the subsequent wave of glorious sludge that was "Only Shallow" penetrated my brain through the store's standard-issue, goofy padded headphones. I remember finding the Japanese import of Radiohead's *Pablo Honey* at the record store where I worked in high school and, through a glitch in the computer system, legally purchasing it for one cent. I remember when my coworker Amanda gave me a burned copy of the Weakerthans' *Reconstruction Site* because I'd told her they reminded me of the obscure Christian band the Waiting. I remember finding a used copy of Midget's *Jukebox* in a record shop in Bath after scouring the United Kingdom for it for nearly two months. It was glorious.

But I have not actually bought an honest-to-God physical CD, one that I was really excited about, in years. Nobody has said to me, out loud, "Man, you've got to hear this," for even longer. Nobody has made me a mix CD for at least five years. It was not so long ago that this was a big part of our world. I'd make mixtapes for, and get them from, girls. I'd hear about a new band from a friend and drive, physically, in a car, to a library, a *building* where they had CDs you could borrow, and I would borrow them, and listen to them carefully, from beginning to end, in my bedroom, and then I would talk, out loud, in person, to my friends about them.

And the experience of buying music, in fact, doesn't feel anything like it used to. Record-store clerks must be starting to feel as useless as the grocery checkers at the supermarket after they put in self-checkout machines. Doing it the human way starts to seem a waste of time; the customer and checker both stare at screens during the transaction, because we know there's no reason to pretend it's a human interaction.

I used to love going to record stores on Tuesdays to find out what was new; the thrill of walking into Sonic Boom Records in Seattle, asking the guy at the desk, "What's the best Built to Spill album?" and then buying it and trusting that it was going to be good because this guy knew what he was talking about. But when I walked into Vancouver's best-known indie record shop a few weeks ago looking for the new Magnetic Fields album, the clerk said, "Oh yeah, I think that's out now." I *knew* it was out, because I'd been reading about its upcoming release on the Internet for *months*, but I was willing to play along. I had been looking forward to the idea of going to a record store to buy a specific record, to strike up a conversation about it, to rip off the plastic, smell the ink and paper of the liner notes. But instead: "Yeah, I guess we just haven't gotten it in yet or something," he said.

What was the point, then? Why not download this album, just like I downloaded the last Magnetic Fields record while I was living in China? I rarely even bought the impossible-to-tell-from-the-originals-except-for-misspellings pirated CDs at my favorite record store in Hangzhou, because it was easier to listen to those records on the computer. I could get a really legit-looking CD of Kayne West's *808s & Heartbreak* for three bucks, or I could listen to it on the Internet for free. It was just easier that way. Easier but a little sadder.

I'm not a curmudgeon.[3] I don't really care that much about format changes in music—I was all for CDs replacing cassettes—and actually, I like the convenience of storing my entire record collection electronically in a plastic box the size of a Bible. I can listen to any song I want without having to spend ten minutes looking for a CD. And yesterday, I downloaded about five records for free—some by friends and people I know, some by artists I've been listening to for years, and some by bands I'd never heard of before who were giving away their music for the sake of giving it away. There is something valuable to be learned from artists who are willing to make gifts of their songs.

I sometimes worry that my memories of music will be forever linked to nostalgia, that I'll keep thinking that the '90s, the decade I really fell in love with music, was the pinnacle of pop music culture, that we were really doing it right back then, there was faith and passion and fun. I don't want it to be like that. I want to still get excited about music, to believe that songs can change everything.

It is still possible, I must remind myself, to do so. Everything I thought I knew and loved in this life, the stuff that made me who I am, came to me between the ages of, roughly, twelve to twenty-four. That was when I learned that I liked school, loved music, wanted to be a Christian, wanted to write. I made records, got married, got

---

3. I totally am.

baptized—and bought thousands of CDs. I have come to see those plastic discs, which I lovingly obsessed over for years, arranging and rearranging, cataloging and alphabetizing, as being encoded with more than music. They are like little pieces of my soul, and I am learning, sometimes painfully, to give them away.

As long as I have been collecting CDs, I have also been getting rid of them—hundreds of them, sometimes even hundreds at a time. During the few years I was getting CDs from music magazines, I'd put together packages of them and mail them to my friends, who would always thank me profusely. I sold a couple of rare Weezer CDs for two dollars to a thirteen-year-old kid at a yard sale, and if he is anything like me, he has fallen in love and has been studying them religiously. I feel the pull of nostalgia each time I get rid of another box of CDs, and I do keep a few (hundred) around, but I've found that giving away an album can be almost as rewarding as getting one.

In a way, I realize that not having physical objects like CDs on hand is a part of my spiritual heritage; we evangelicals have always eschewed the beautiful cathedrals, the "bells and smells," in favor of what most of us would call "what really matters." Things matter, sure. I'll buy my favorite bands' new records when they come out. But each time I give away something I care about, I feel some sort of intangible benefit to my soul, which somehow feels a little lighter. You don't have to own something to "get something" from it. Shifting music from physical to digital media underscores this truth, in a way. Songs, like all things, come into and out of our lives like wind and rain, and to have enjoyed them for a time is enough.

WHAT I WRITE ABOUT WHEN I WRITE ABOUT MUSIC AND RELIGION

I have been writing about the intersection of pop music and religion for almost as long as I can remember: since I was fifteen, making top-ten lists and reviewing Newsboys concerts in zines that were never published, to last week, when I e-mailed a publicist about interviewing Sixpence None the Richer. Music and faith are twin passions of mine; they will always be who I am. Life for me can't be anything other than a spiritual and—as Larry Mullen Jr. says in U2's *Rattle and*

Hum documentary—"musical journey." I am still at it and will keep writing about it.

I like to write about bands who are what Greg Wolfe, editor of the religious literary journal *Image*, calls "grapplers," bands who wrestle with faith and belief. Some are professing people of faith, some are not, and most are not involved with "Christian music."

Sometimes I get into trouble because of this. Bands that flit around the dark edges of faith tend to be anxious about being associated with CCM and the evangelical Christian subculture. When the words *Christian* and *music* get too close to each other in a sentence, they create all kinds of weird, unpleasant associations, and no serious artist, even one in a medium as allegedly commercial and ephemeral as pop music, wants anybody to think that their records should be shelved alongside Sandi Patty and Carman.

When I write about these grapplers, I tread lightly, because I am pulling for them; I, too, would prefer less cultural isolation and fewer lines drawn in the sand when it comes to this stuff. Yet I am genuinely interested in not only how faith and pop music work together, but also how the cultural implications play out: I really *do* want to know what makes somebody choose to sign to, say, Tooth & Nail Records, and then what makes them want to jump ship. I want to know why former singers of Christian metal bands become atheists. I want to explain how a song about a yeti is actually a song about the power of belief ("Bigfoot!" by the Weakerthans). And so I run into problems.

I've seen letters to the editor calling me stupid for making fun of Christian culture. I've gotten incoherent blog comments that suggested I didn't know the Bible as well as I should or that the band I'd lovingly written a thousand-word elegy for had "denied Christ" because they went mainstream. I've had bands back out of interviews because I asked too many questions about religion.

Recently, I had a fifteen–e-mail tête-à-tête with a band's manager who didn't want me to write about the group for a Christian magazine because, he wrote, they had worked very hard to keep the band's name away from anything approaching CCM. They had built a positive reputation in a very specific subgenre of modern music and were not about to jeopardize it by being mentioned in a publication that might let slip that they were a Christian grunge band ten years ago.

The band epitomized the theme of my piece, and to write the article without them would be irresponsible. I told the manager as much in an e-mail and essentially threatened to mention the band whether they wanted to talk to me or not. They gave the interview, and although I don't expect you'll be seeing mention of it on the band's Web site any time soon, I'm glad it worked out.

I am drawn to the nexus of faith and pop music because they both seem to get at the same thing. Religion seeks to explain the big human dilemmas, and it gives shape to the answers. Rock music seeks a way of living the questions—a process, a movement, that is full of body and sound and urgency. I love both of these things, and writing is how I figure things out, so in a sense I write about this stuff to indulge myself in a quest to keep figuring stuff out.

But another reason I write about music and faith is that I suspect I'm not the only one who cares about it and that, as much fun as it is to wax rapturous and jokey about the records I grew up with, I want to help push things forward. The existence of CCM has made us lazy when it comes to music—if you're a fan of Christian music you can slide by without ever really paying attention to what you're putting into your head through your ears, even if it's really bad for you.

I was just saying a few pages ago (remember?) that I want to do something with this spirit of giving when it comes to music, and writing about it is the best way I know how. So I want to keep writing about this, when I can, to remind everybody, my fellow former and current and future evangelical Christians, that we are going to have to keep our ears awake. We do not need Christian record companies or magazines or retailers to tell us what is safe to listen to, to tell us which bands and artists have more faith than others or which ones are *really* Christians and worthy of our support. The time for that is over.

We need a network, a cloud of mp3-blogging witnesses, word of mouth and grassroots efforts, individual writers and critics and blogs and zines and scenes who are guided by the faith, hope, and love we have in Christ. I think all I want is to be a tiny part of that.

My motivation for writing about music has changed over the years. I wanted to be cool. I wanted to get free swag. I wanted to show that I was smart. I wanted to interview my favorite bands. I wanted to explore cultural phenomena. But what has remained constant, and what is most important to me now, is that I write about music because it has always filled me with inexplicable joy, a joy I can only say comes from God, and I want to share that with everyone I know. Now if you'll excuse me, I need to go turn up the stereo, strap on my guitar, and rock out.

FIVE ALBUMS I COULDN'T FIT INTO ANY OTHER CHAPTER BUT WHICH I REALLY LOVE AND MIGHT EVEN STILL BE LISTENING TO WHEN I AM OLD

 mewithoutYou, *Brother, Sister* (Tooth & Nail, 2006)

mewithoutYou has made four records (as of this writing), and in eight years they have evolved from a raucous post–hard-core/ screamo band to an Americana-influenced indie pop group. They're also one of the most compellingly religious bands in recent memory, rooted in Christianity but heavily influenced by Judaism, Islam, and Sufism. *Brother, Sister* acts as a gateway from the straining spoken-word epics of their early work to the pastoral, folksy direction they began moving in afterward, with detours into psychedelia and dub on the title track. Aaron Weiss sings, slurs, mumbles, and screams over this hypnotic post-punk, and by the time he is shouting "Allahu Akbar" over some sinister-sounding bass riffs, I start wondering how Tooth & Nail agreed to put this out at all. You have not heard rock & roll transcendence until you have heard Jeremy Enigk, a guest vocalist on this album, screaming, "That light is God!" over Weiss's humble poetry and the band's frenetic pummeling.

 Sixpence None the Richer, *Sixpence None the Richer* (Squint, 1997)

Sixpence None the Richer is the album that both jump-started and sabotaged the band's career, thanks mostly to the eventual mega-hit status of "Kiss Me" and the pressure and fame it brought them. But before it was anything like that (the record actually came out two years before the "Kiss Me" mania started), it was just a gorgeous pop record about the struggle between art and commerce, between loving and being unlovable, between Sixpence and the music business. I always tell people I could write pages and pages about why I love this band and this album, but I have never been able to actually do it. Maybe it's because every note feels so perfectly placed, Steve Taylor's crystalline production so crisp, that I don't think I could add anything to it. Sixpence recently reunited, and my confidence in them is such that I am 100 percent certain their new record will be good.

The Prayer Chain, *Mercury* (Rode Dog, 1995)

This album is truly one of the lost classics of the '90s, or maybe the entire modern rock era, easily on par with the other much-feted ethereal classics—your Jeff Buckleys, your Cocteau Twins, what have you. Suddenly out of nowhere came this otherworldly drone of "Humb," *Mercury*'s first track. This drone sounds like something between a forest and a didgeridoo but is probably a guitar played through a hundred different effects pedals; it's later joined by a smooth, gentle, fluid, insistent bass line that pushes the song so gently along as Tim Taber (who all the other band members hated, according to interviews about that period) sings from Psalm 100, "His lovingkindness is neverending." The rest of the record takes off from there through endless drones, reverb, weird percussion, and faraway vocals. It's a record of songs about decay and numbness and sex (really!), which finally ends where it began, with the drone and bass line of "Humb" turning into the epic finale "Sun Stoned." A liberal estimate would be that less than one-tenth of one percent of the world's population has heard of it. Please buy it immediately. I'll wait.

Moxy Früvous, *Bargainville* (WEA/Atlantic, 1994)

I would prefer not to admit that my musical consciousness owes a great deal to an album by a Canadian novelty folk vocal group whose music belongs on a spectrum somewhere between the Barenaked Ladies and Weird Al. So I won't. I'll just mention that I don't know anyone outside my immediate family who has heard this album, which is a real shame, because it's full of smart songs, lovely harmonies, crystal-clear vocals, jokes, and tearjerkers. "My Baby Loves a Bunch of Authors" was allegedly the first Canadian number-one single by a Canadian band, which makes sense to me, because it's a very sharp and literary and polished song, and Canada is a very sharp and polished and literary country. I mostly dug the joke songs—"King of Spain" in particular, about a king who decides to swap places with a peasant—but I now see the deep poignancy in the songs about death, drinking, and war that pepper this album. (Fortunately, however, it ends with a cover of the "Spiderman" theme.)

Danielson, *Ships* (Secretly Canadian, 2006)

Danielson, like many of the non-CCM Christian bands I've started to know and love in recent years, is a really weird band that few people have heard of and many people dislike. I can see why— I didn't like them at first either—since the focus of the group is Daniel Smith's piglet-squeal vocals, delivered in childish yelps, and the instruments often sound like they're being played by a group of enthusiastic eight-year-olds, but *Ships* is an incredibly cohesive, joyous, lively record, full of raucous experimentation and pop-genius simplicity. "Did I Step On Your Trumpet?" is among the greatest pop songs I have heard, and its themes of forgiveness, generosity, and acceptance are carried through to the album's final song, which concludes in a cacophony of instrumental improv where the family (Smith's brothers, sisters, wife, children, and parents are all involved in his musical life to some degree) sings "thanks / thanks / thanks / thanks / thanks / thanks / THAAAAAAANKS!" I can't think of a better reason to write a song.

Discussion Questions for Your Bible Study, Ladies' Tea, or Heavy Metal Vomit Party[1]

1. Did you notice the way in which the author jumps from treating the relationship between popular music and the Christian faith with great dignity and seriousness to treating it like a big joke? Is this itself a symptom of evangelical Christian culture? Discuss.

2. What is the worst Christian pop song you have ever heard? Hint: if you did not choose "Cartoons" by Chris Rice, you are wrong.

3. Did you notice a distinct lack of talk about rap, R & B, gospel, and other historically black music in this book? Do you think that is because the author is a narrow-minded small-town white boy, or because the CCM industry tends to sell a lot more white artists' records than black artists' records?

4. To be fair, Eminem sells tons of records, so it's not like this is only a Christian thing, but surely you have noticed that Christian music's most well-known rapper is a white guy from Tennessee?

5. This book notwithstanding, is it possible to successfully marry thoughtful music criticism with autobiography, even if the author has not led a particularly interesting life?

6. When was the moment you lost *your* faith in Christian music? Did it in any way involve Carman's "Witch's Invitation"?

---

1. Apologies to John Hughes (RIP).

7. How many times have you seen dc Talk in concert? In an essay, describe, citing relevant theories of aesthetics, how you felt when they stopped using backup dancers.

8. How many concerts have you been to that had altar calls?

9. How many concerts have you been to that had altar calls that you went up for?

10. Say, have you ever heard of Jesus?

11. Would you like to know more about Jesus?

12. Would you like to read this delightful pamphlet about Jesus, rendered in comic-book form, which brazenly insults your intelligence and attempts to scare you into becoming a fundamentalist Christian, even if you are already another kind of Christian?

13. How many times have you asked Jesus into your heart, *really*?

14. Doing it once more couldn't hurt, right?[2]

15. Have you been baptized?

16. How many times?[3]

17. What are some reasons you should burn your entire non-Christian record collection? List as many as you can.

18. How long did it take you to find and replace all those non-Christian records you got rid of, and how much money did it cost you? Do you feel like an idiot, or what?

19. Is it wrong to use a file-sharing network to download a Christian worship album, such as the David Crowder Band's *A Collision*?

20. Are you sure? Even if at the time you were in a country that has fairly lax copyright protection standards and everyone else you knew was downloading way more music and movies than you were, and theirs wasn't even Christian?

21. Fact: There has been a robust Contemporary Christian Music industry for thirty years, but there has never been a Contemporary Christian Movie industry of comparable size or cultural impact. Why, exactly, is that?

2. This sentence was actually said to me by a street evangelist once.
3. See note 2.

22. A lot of people have told me that this difference is because movies cost a lot more to make, so I guess it's just that we can tolerate making a lot of subpar Christian records for $50,000 each, but we can't tolerate making a lot of subpar Christian movies at $50 million each? If that's the reason they don't make more *Left Behind* movies, that's cool, but is it really that simple?

23. And also, it seems like almost nobody in the Christian media takes "non-Christian" music seriously, but they take "non-Christian" movies seriously. What's the deal?

24. List five records you think everybody who is serious about Christian faith and pop music should listen to.

25. Now flip through the reviews of records put forward by the author at the end of each chapter, compare them to yours, and see if you were right.

26. Did you notice that the author never really figured out whether this book was about "Christian music" or just "music and Christianity"? Is that kind of the whole point, or was he simply confused? Is there a difference?

27. Were there times when you felt like throwing this book across the room because the author was so clearly wrong about something, like when he made fun of your favorite band, or when he praised a worthless record to high heaven? If so, does that mean the author did his job well, or is he a stupid jerk?

28. Recall the notion of the "un-scene" mentioned in the first chapter. After reading the rest of the book, did you feel that there was, in fact, almost nothing of real substance mentioned, and it was just page after page of somebody's *opinions* and *feelings* about pop-culture ephemera rather than actual, meaningful life stories? Is this a problem for you to the point that it will keep you from recommending this book to your friends? Would you mind keeping that to yourself?

29. Was the use of the term "un-scene" in fact a veiled attempt by the author to promote his unpopular blog of the same name, which currently gets about ten unique visitors per day, many of whom are family members or people looking for an mp3 of "Jesus Walk with Me" by Club 8, which is a fantastic song?

30. The author claims there is no such thing as Catholic rock, but he is probably wrong. Can you think of some examples of Catholic rock bands?

31. Where did Switchfoot go wrong?

32. Where did Sixpence None the Richer go wrong?

33. Where did Jars of Clay go wrong?

34. Where did Creed go wrong?[4]

35. A friend of the author who did not grow up in the evangelical subculture compared certain sections of this book to "reading a movie review of a movie I haven't seen." If you also did not grow up in the evangelical subculture, do you agree or disagree?

36. If you were the author's sister, would you be disappointed that you were hardly mentioned at all, especially given that music is actually a way bigger part of your life than of the author's?

37. If you are the author's wife, are you sick yet of hearing him talk about "my book" all the time? Because this will all be over soon, I swear.

4. This is a trick question, because it assumes they went right at some point.

Rock Band Index

* Artists whose names appear in bold are featured in end-of-chapter reviews.